Dire Straits

Social and Economic Studies No. 43
Institute of Social and Economic Research
Memorial University of Newfoundland

Dire Straits:
The Dilemmas of a Fishery

The Case of Digby Neck and the Islands

Anthony Davis

ISER

**Institute of Social and
Economic Research**

© Institute of Social and Economic Research
Memorial University of Newfoundland
St. John's, Newfoundland
Canada
ISBN 0-919666-64-7
1991

Printed on paper
containing over 50%
recycled paper including
5% post-consumer fibre.

Canadian Cataloguing in Publication Data

Davis, Anthony, 1950-

  Dire straits

  (Social and economic studies, ISSN 0847-0898 ;
no. 43)

  Includes bibliographical references.
  ISBN 0-919666-64-7

1. Fisheries -- Economic aspects -- Nova Scotia --
Digby Neck Region. 2. Fisheries -- Social
aspects -- Nova Scotia -- Digby Neck Region.
3. Digby Neck Region (N.S.) -- Economic conditions.
4. Digby Neck Region (N.S.) -- Social conditions.
I. Memorial University of Newfoundland. Institute of
Social and Economic Research. II. Title.
III. Series: Social and economic studies (St.
John's, Nfld.) ; no. 43.

SH224.N6D38 1991 338.3'727'0971632 C91-097604-X

This book is dedicated to, James Soper, a courageous fellow traveller and good friend with the nerve to follow his interest and, in so doing, spread the word about anthropology; and to my family, Audrey, Kathryn and Parnell—the glue, the centre, the meaning.

Contents

Acknowledgements xi

Preface xiii

1 Introduction 1

2 Location and Environment 4

3 A Profile of the Fishing Industry 15

4 The Development of the Small Boat
Dragger Fleet 38

5 The Impact of Small Boat Draggers
on the Digby Neck and Islands Fishery 46

6 Fish Draggers and Fish Buyers:
Systemic Connections in the
Transformation of the Fishery 61

7 Government Interventions:
The Drive to Industrialise the Fisheries 71

8 Conclusion 87

Appendix 100

Notes 103

References 108

ISER Books 112

List of Tables

1 Population by Place for Digby Neck
   and the Islands Community Areas,
   1966, 1971, 1981   13

2 Motorised Boats, <10 Tons and >10 Tons,
   Digby Neck and the Islands (District 37),
   1953–1972   28

3 Motorised Boats by Length and Sector
   (Coastal Zone/Offshore), Digby Neck and the
   Islands (District 37), 1979–1983   28

4 Number of Fishermen, Number of Boats,
   Average Number of Fishermen per Boat,
   Digby Neck and the Islands (District 37),
   Selected Years Between 1953–1983   30

5 Landed Weights (000's lbs.) and Landed Values
   ($000) for Selected Groundfish Species,
   Digby Neck and the Islands (District 37),
   1952–1983   49

6 Coastal Zone Landings as a % of Total Landed
   Weights for Selected Groundfish Species,
   Digby Neck and the Islands (District 37),
   1967–1983   51

7 Coastal Zone Herring Landings as a %
   of Total Herring Landings, (000's lbs.)
   Digby Neck and the Islands (District 37),
   1967–1983   52

8 Landed Weights (000's lbs.) and Landed
   Values ($000) for Lobster, Digby Neck
   and the Islands (District 37), 1952–1983   53

9 Fleet Structure by Selected Communities,
   Digby Neck and the Islands (District 37)
   for Various Years between 1957–1983   55

10 Number of Fishermen by Status
   in Selected Communities, Digby Neck and
   the Islands (District 37) for Various Years   57

11 Number of Fishing Licences Issued by
   Selected Specific Fisheries, Digby Neck
   and the Islands (District 37), 1963–1983   78

List of Maps

1   Digby Neck and the Islands   5
2   The Distribution of Cod and Haddock   8
3   The Distribution of Pollock and Herring   9
4   Coastal Zone Fishing Grounds   18
5   Offshore Fishing Grounds   27

List of Figures

1   The Cape Island Boat   16
2   Coastal Zone Fishing Technologies   20
3   The Small Boat Dragger   23
4   The Otter Trawl   24

Acknowledgements

The research for this study was supported by a grant from the Social Sciences and Humanities Research Council of Canada. St. Mary's University through the Office of the Dean of Arts and the Gorsebrook Research Institute also facilitated the research by providing essential support services. My project colleagues, Richard Apostle and Gene Barrett, provided consistent encouragement and useful suggestions. Leonard Kasdan's assistance and guidance throughout the research and report drafting processes were invaluable. He joined me in the field, offering key suggestions and insights. His store house of source knowledge contributed directly to the outline of the manuscript and to the development of the 'story' contained in the observational, interview and quantitative data that was gathered. Leonard Kasdan also took the lead in drafting Chapters Two and Three for the research report developed from this project. In short, this work would have taken a different course had it not been for his contributions.

Ms. Janice Raymond, Economics Branch, Department of Fisheries and Oceans, Halifax office provided us with valuable assistance and information. The manuscript was prepared originally by Ms. Donna Edwards, a fisher's daughter and extraordinary interpreter/typist. To her I owe many thanks for her patience, persistence and encouragement. I have been blessed with the good fortune of having Mrs. Frances Baker of Antigonish and her many skills available to me for re-processing of the manuscript and enthusiastic encouragement through various stages. I am also grateful for the helpful comments from reviewers and Ian McKay, Gorsebrook Research Institute. Without the encouragement and enthusiasm of Ms. Susan Nichol, Assistant Editor, as well as the support and effort of ISER Books, this manuscript would never have seen the light of day.

Of course, this work could not have been done without the willingness of many people in the Digby Neck, Long Island, and Brier Island area to share their experiences, thoughts and concerns with me. I hope they find that this book is an accurate and useful portrait of their industry and livelihoods.

This book has been published with the help of a grant from the Social Science Federation of Canada, using funds provided by the Social Sciences and Humanities Research Council of Canada.

Preface

This book tells the story of a fishery situated in Digby Neck and the Islands, Nova Scotia, that has been undergoing tremendous changes over the last three decades. It charts major characteristics of these changes, describing the parts played by dominant figures in the fishery and related industries, and observes the present condition of the industry as well as predicting its probable contribution to the area's future economy. In many ways the Digby Neck and the Islands fishing industry conforms with popular notions of the course of technological and economic development necessary for the Atlantic Canadian fishery to become viable and self-supporting.[1] This is a regional fishery that has experienced extensive technological modernisation and reorganisation. Yet, as this study shows, increasing technological sophistication and capitalisation have contributed to the appearance of profound problems in, and dilemmas for, the industry. The research reported here was carried out in the summer of 1984 as the case study component of a project funded by the Social Sciences and Humanities Research Council of Canada called "Land and Sea: The Structure of Fish Processing in Nova Scotia." This project was concerned with examining various factors contributing to the survival and proliferation of small- and intermediate-scale fish processing enterprises in Nova Scotia. It focused upon fish plant managers, fish plant workers and the captains of vessels which supply these plants. Since the social and economic factors in the communities in which this sector of the industry operates are important to the fishery, it was decided to study a Nova Scotia regional fishery in detail.

The major aims of the research project were: (1) to examine the relationship between community conditions of labour surplus and location, choice of technique, production process and restructuring in the processing sector; (2) to examine the relationship between resource access—the type and quality of species utilized, the types of fishers relied upon and the nature of the ties between fishers and processors, product-niche, seasonality—and production structure in the processing sector; (3) to examine the qualitative dimensions of human attachment to the fishing industry in communities where the processing sector varies according to scale and ownership type; and (4) to examine the centrality and depth of marketing ties between fish processors and brokers of various sorts, especially in the New England market. In pursuit of these aims a survey of fish plant managers/owners was carried out in the summer of 1984.[2] Since the community-based supply aspects were not thoroughly covered by the survey it was necessary to conduct a contextually-based study which would concentrate on community and regional aspects of the industry, particularly the relationship between fleet structure, the processing sector, and port market dynamics. To this end the communities of the Digby Neck and the Islands area of Southwestern Nova Scotia were chosen for field study. This area is particularly appropriate for a number of reasons. First, its communities have a long history of exclusive dependence upon the fishery as the basis of their economy. Without exception they are single-sector communities. Consequently, community organisation and vitality were anticipated to be particularly sensitive to and reflective of conditions in the industry. A second reason for choosing this area was the existence of an extensive baseline study that had been completed over two decades earlier.[3] I anticipated that this could be drawn upon for purposes of studying socio-economic change. Another consideration was that Southwest Nova Scotia contains a disproportionate share of the province's processing plants, fishers, fishing vessels and fishery generated income. In addition, I had already carried out extensive field research in the Cape Sable Island area. Thus the Digby Neck and Islands study provided an opportunity both to test the generality of some established knowledge as well as to expand upon our understanding of the Southwest Nova Scotia fisheries.

A NOTE ON METHODOLOGY

Research was undertaken during the months of June through August, 1984 in the Digby Neck and Islands area. The village of Tiverton was used as a base of operation, and interviews and participant observation were used to document the structure and dynamics of the fishery as it is presently constituted as well as to outline the transformations it has undergone.

Data and observations were gathered in a variety of ways. Since the research was intended to provide a regional study animated by participant-observation, I spent some time going on fishing trips with hook-and-line and dragger fishers. Information gathered in this manner, i.e., observations and informal interviews, was recorded in field notes. The same procedure was used following the numerous informal conversations with fishers, fish plant workers and community workers.

In addition to unstructured information gathering, I also completed a considerable number of in-depth, taped interviews with fishers currently engaged, on a full-time basis, in the coastal zone and small boat dragger fisheries. These interviews reflected both opportunistic and intentional selection. On the one hand, I interviewed any fishers who were receptive to my request for an interview (not all were). On the other hand, I sought and obtained interviews with the particular individuals whose names kept coming up in conversations whenever the topics of dragger fishing and success were broached. Contentious and suspect information was cross-checked with a couple of individuals with whom I had developed a key informant relationship.

In-depth, taped interviews were also completed with seven owners/managers of the local fish plants. These interviews questioned the owners/managers about every aspect of their business, ranging from relations with fishers and equity involvement with small boat fish draggers through the size and characteristics of their labour force, particular characteristics of their business organisation, relations with the fish companies and market connections. The information gathered here, plus untaped informal conversations held with a number of the buyers, both following the interviews and on other occasions, added tremendously to our understanding of the developmental history and current socio-economic dynamics of fish buying and processing within this region.

Formal and informal interviews with a number of current and retired fisheries officers and fishers also proved invaluable to my reconstruction of recent developments and trends, especially following World War II, in this region's fisheries. One of these fisheries officers was gracious enough to summarise key points in the Annual Narrative Reports, documents written by local fisheries officers and submitted, on an annual basis, to the Department of Fisheries and Oceans. These Reports contain the senior fisheries officers' perceptions of developments in and problems facing the region's fisheries as experienced on location. As such, the summaries have proven critical to documenting changes in the structure and dynamics of the industry, especially as these relate to the rise of small boat dragger fishing. Needless to say, I owe endless thanks to the officer who expended the time, effort and care in providing the summaries. He adhered to my requests concerning documentation of information provided (e.g., year of report and page number) and left me satisfied concerning the diligence of his efforts to provide information in the topic areas I specified (e.g., observations on changes in fleet structure, number of participants, changes in landings, economic shifts, conflict etc.). Finally, Department of Fisheries and Oceans, Scotia-Fundy Office, graciously provided me with specific, detailed longitudinal information regarding ocean resource landings, licences, numbers of participants in the industry, fleet characteristics and so on.

Specific number data, related experiences, observations and the like, obtained in the ways outlined above, constitute the information base out of which we have come to understand the Digby Neck and the Islands fisheries as they are discussed in the following text. From the outset my intent was to complete a case study largely informed by anthropological field methods, e.g., participant-observations, informal conversations and extensive use of key informants. Structured, taped interviewing was employed selectively and opportunistically with the exception of my work with fish plant owners and managers. All comments presented in the text as direct quotations were obtained during taped interviews. This study does not reflect sociological prescriptions for statistical validity/representativeness. Nonetheless, my time with these people, although relatively brief in duration, a little less than four months, resulted in a wealth of qualitatively rich information that revealed the structure and dynamic of the Digby Neck and the Islands fisheries.

While intending a more anthropological focus in methods, analyses and 'feel,' early observations brought a change in the perspective and writing of analysis altogether. These observations caused me to shift away from a case study approach and to focus on regional dimensions. It quickly became apparent that the fishery was in a serious crisis and that this crisis was the result of a closely interrelated set of factors. These factors were: (1) changes in fish catching and fish processing technologies; (2) the socio-economic and ecological impact of these changes; (3) a recent social and economic re-organisation of the area's fishing industry, and (4) the impact of government policy on the above. The study which follows documents these relationships and interprets their impact upon the social and economic topography of Digby Neck and the Islands.

Introduction **1**

Most of the morning's fog had burnt off but a grey veil still shrouded the buildings, the wharf, the vessels and the people as Mr. Clarence and I strolled along the main road through Tiverton.[1] Mr. Clarence, now 68, had fished out of this place all his life. He started at fourteen with his father's brother, and was in his early twenties before he got a boat of his own. His had been a life of handline, longline, lobster and herring net fishing, and he had fished year-round until unemployment insurance came in. Although his income had been low and the work hard, Mr. Clarence insisted that his life had been satisfying. After all, he had always worked and lived among kin and familiars. Through his life here Mr. Clarence had seen many changes—particularly since the coming of the dragger.[2] As we walked along the harbour front, Mr. Clarence told me of the way things used to be in Tiverton:

> At one time practically everyone with a boat had a shack and a place on the shore. Here or down at Pirate's Cove. You know, we'd keep our gear and stuff in there. We'd also have it as a place to work in, fixin' up traps and line, mendin' nets, baitin' gear. We were always visitin' one and another. Sittin' and chewin' about this or that. Most of those places are gone now. A lot of 'em were taken durin' the Ground Hog Day Storm, back in '76. Many of 'em had been abandoned by then anyways and were well on their way to collapsin'. Oh, at one time this place was filled with boats comin' and goin'. People busy. Always a lot of activity then.

Mr. Clarence also spoke of how many people used to put up their own fish, splitting and salting cod and hake in their sheds to be sold "green," right out of pickle, in order to get a higher price from the buyers.

Further along the road stood the remains of a building and a wharf which had been larger than most. Mr. Clarence explained that it was once the site of a good-sized fish plant:

Here they used to put up a lot of fish. It was quite a business at one time. There used to be a number of saltin' businesses all along here. Small and large. Of course salt fish was the thing then, not fresh like now. Used to make a lot of work for people here abouts, at least for part of the year. Now most of 'em's gone. All that's left are the pilin's and a few of the old buildings.

As we walked along the paved cap of the expansive government wharf, Mr. Clarence paused and waved at the couple of small boat fish draggers tied up alongside: "A lot of things have changed around here since they came in, a lot of things, and not many of them good, if you ask me."

This volume profiles and analyses the character and consequences of the changes to the Digby Neck and the Islands fisheries. I originally intended to focus my research on fish buyer-fisher socio-economic relationships within selected port markets, but instead I studied the regional-level processes and outcomes connected with the adoption of the small boat fish dragger. This occurred for two reasons. Firstly, the fishers I interviewed revealed that the focus of fisher-fishbuyer relationships within the Digby Neck and the Islands fishery was situated in the relation between fish draggers and fish processing companies. Secondly, early in my field research I discovered that the occupational and social communities on Digby Neck and the Islands were fragmented to a degree I had not expected. This fragmentation was an apparent outcome of the rise to predominance of the small boat fish dragger within the region's fishery.

Consequently, I decided to concentrate on documenting the connection of the small boat fish dragger to the changes in, and contemporary characteristics of, Digby Neck and the Islands social and economic life. I suspected that this might reveal the dynamics of the port market. I also sensed that such a focus would permit me the opportunity to present a detailed study of the socio-economic consequences of technical modernisation within a particular fishery, especially since the Digby Neck and the Islands case represented the sort of ideal implicit in much of the federal government's fisheries policies. By design, this study emphasises largely regional-level, socio-economic dynamics; I do not examine specific cases of the responses and/or opposition of fishers and communities to the processes and changes I have documented. Published material from earlier research in the region relates and analyses details of these processes (Hughes *et al.* 1960; Richardson 1952), but a contemporary study of similar focus remains, and needs, to be done.

It has not been my intention in choosing a more regional focus to ignore or underestimate the importance of human dynamics and responses within local-level social and economic organisation. To the contrary, my emphasis on regional-level analyses is intended to reveal the power relations rooted in both the local social structure and the broader society, which continue to determine the quality of life for many on Digby Neck and the Islands. This emphasis seems essential to an understanding of the failure of resistance to socio-economic change.

This focus has afforded me the opportunity to examine intended and perhaps unintended consequences of federal government fisheries management policies. The federal government, empowered to dictate the terms and conditions of resource supply and trade, determines much of the socio-economic organisation and development of fish production and processing. Throughout this volume I have given particular attention to the historical intersection of governmental management practices and development initiatives, with the economic interests and entrepreneurial behaviour of certain Digby Neck and the Islands fishers and fish processors. While state policy may not be designed with specific individuals in mind, it does contribute largely to the shape and conditions of opportunity available to social and economic communities. The tale told within these pages is, in no small measure, about the ways in which government policies have intersected with particular elements and interests in Digby Neck and the Islands social structure, thereby enabling a transformation of the fishing industry that has reached into every aspect of local-level life. In part, I see the conditions described and analysed herein as symptomatic of the changes underway throughout Atlantic Canada's fishing industry, although different regions and places are situated at various stages in the transformation vortex. In my judgement, the dilemmas identified and discussed are inescapable outcomes of the determination of change as it has been directed and overseen by government policy, and by those well positioned within local social structure to reap the benefits. But these dilemmas are the outcome of *one* path of social and economic development. I am convinced that other paths, more sensitive and responsive to local priorities, potentials and dynamics, would realise different outcomes.

Location and Environment 2

This study covers the Digby Neck and Long Island and Brier Island areas of Digby County in southwest Nova Scotia.[1] Before describing the primary location of interest, a more general description is necessary to place the area in socio-historical and environmental context. This part of Nova Scotia is profoundly affected by its location between the Bay of Fundy on one side and St. Mary's Bay on the other. St. Mary's Bay is a sub-unit of the Bay of Fundy. It forms an arm of the bay running in a northeast to southwest direction. St. Mary's Bay is separated from the Bay of Fundy on its northwest side by Digby Neck and the Islands. Its other boundary is the south-western mainland of Nova Scotia (see Map 1).

THE MAINLAND SIDE OF ST. MARY'S BAY

The mainland side is characterised by a broad, low area of glacial origin marked by few large harbours, but it contains a number of coves which have been the focal point of European, especially French, settlement. Here an adaptation developed which combined a primary orientation to the sea with seasonal subsistence farming and the exploitation of the woodlands which stretched into the higher inland areas of the region.

The French Acadian settlers, and their descendants in this area, developed a pluralistic adaptation. The primary exploitation of the marine, agricultural and forest resources gave rise to secondary industries based on these resources. Wooden ship building and fish processing completed the pluralistic adaptation of the mainland area of the bay. The settlement pattern characteristic of the area is a dispersed one, with houses stretched along the road which runs parallel to the shores of the bay. The lands associated with these houses are at right angles to shore and road. Thus even those

Map 1

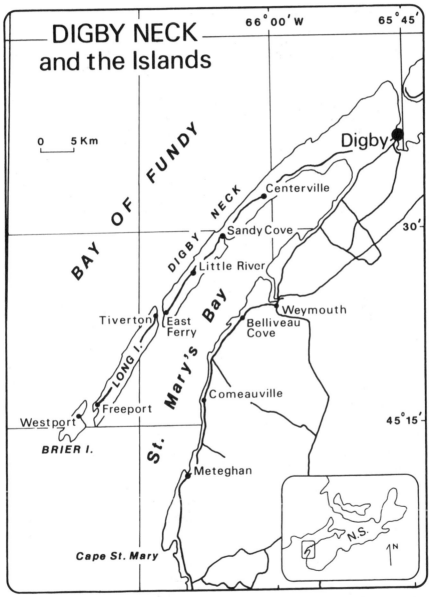

Cartographer: Austin Rodgers

housed further inland have access to the bay, agricultural land and forest.

THE DIGBY NECK AND ISLANDS AREA

Digby Neck juts out into the Bay of Fundy in a southwesterly direction, defining the northwest boundary of St. Mary's Bay. The neck is broken by two gaps: Petit Passage which sets off Long Island from Digby Neck proper, and Grand Passage which separates Long Island from Brier Island. Digby Neck is a long narrow basalt ridge composed of triassic trap rock. Soils derived from these formations are too shallow and stony for agriculture. In some areas the soils are even too shallow to support extensive forest cover. "Where there is sufficient soil, white spruce, maple, fir, birch and poplar grow well. Where the soil is very thin vegetation is stunted or limited ... " (Hichley *et al.* 1962:27). In general, Digby Neck is not productive enough to have become a lumbering area, although in the past it has provided some wood products for local use.

Given the area's inadequacies for agriculture and forestry, it is not surprising that, Digby Neck's communities, in contrast to those of the mainland, rely almost exclusively upon marine resources for their survival. Fortunately, the Bay of Fundy is one of the most productive marine resource areas to be found anywhere. A combination of climatic and geographical conditions explain this great productivity. Located at a latitude which in Europe would provide a Mediterranean climate, the Bay of Fundy region is characterised by a humid, temperate climate which is buffered from extremes of temperature in both summer and winter. The weather station closest to Digby Neck reports a temperature range over a 22-year-period fluctuating from a mean winter low of 26°F to a mean summer high of 59°F. Precipitation is fairly evenly distributed throughout the year. Of the mean average of 40.6 inches, 11.2 inches fall in the winter, 8.6 in the spring, 9.5 in the summer and 11.3 in the fall (Hichley *et al.* 1962:9).

There are two major influences upon the climate of the Bay of Fundy: the Labrador current which follows the coast of Nova Scotia and terminates in the Bay of Fundy, and the bay itself, which is influenced by seasonal flows of warm air borne on the prevailing southwesterly winds. These influences, when interacting with the cooler air accompanying the Labrador current, frequently create fogs in the bay in the warmer months. The fact that this climatic regime delays the warm season in summer and buffers the bay from extreme low temperatures in winter makes it possible to exploit marine resources on a year-round basis. This contrasts with the more marked seasonal patterns of other areas in Nova Scotia and Atlantic Canada.

The Bay of Fundy has some of the highest tides in the world. The tides, when combined with the mixing and upwelling of the Bay of Fundy—Gulf of Maine region, lead to unsurpassed productivity in marine resources, providing a rich seasonal nutrient mix, leading to blooms of the phyto-plankton and zooplankton upon which a variety of fish stocks depend.

Both the nearshore and distant water fleets are particularly well located for the exploitation of a variety of marine resources, including fish and shellfish. A variety of stocks are seasonally available to the fishing communities of southwest Nova Scotia and Digby Neck. Stocks of cod, haddock, pollock, hake and herring move close to these areas during their migratory cycles (see Maps 2 and 3). In addition, the high value lobster resource is available in the winter months.

THE DIGBY NECK AND THE ISLANDS COMMUNITIES

In contrast to the Acadian communities which stretch down the other side of St. Mary's Bay, and have a linear settlement pattern along the main road, the communities on Digby Neck and the Islands show a more clustered settlement pattern. Frame wooden houses overlook a cove or other protected anchorage, and are located with social access to kin and neighbors. Typically, the shoreline is lined with storage sheds ("stores") for gear and bait, each with a wooden wharf standing on high wooden piles, above the limits of the extreme tides. When these communities are approached from the sea, the shoreline appears completely lined with these sheds and wharves, with the exception of the larger concrete and stone government wharves. A roadway parallels the line of sheds, and the first cluster of houses faces the sheds across this road. Additional paths and roads wind up the surrounding hillsides and give access to other clusters of homes.

In addition to the individually owned stores on the shoreline, one or more large buildings stand on pilings jutting out into the water. Many of these are, or were, fish processing facilities. Here the catches are transformed into various products for outside markets. In the past a variety of products were produced by a multiplicity of smaller plants. Many of these are no longer in existence. As a testament to this past, along the waterfronts of many of these communities, there are usually one or more derelict plants in various stages of decay.

Map 2: Distribution of Cod and Haddock

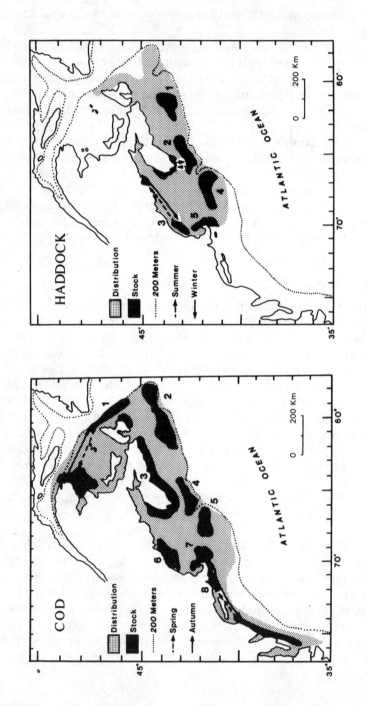

Cartography by Austin Rodgers, from a map in G.M. Hare, *Atlas of the Major Atlantic Coast Fish and Invertebrate Resource Adjacent to the Canada-United States Boundary Areas.*

Map 3: Distribution of Pollock and Herring

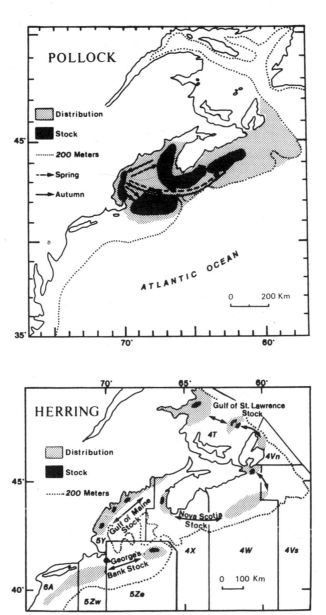

Cartography by Austin Rodgers, from a map in G.M. Hare, *Atlas of the Major Atlantic Coast Fish and Invertebrate Resource Adjacent to the Canada-United States Boundary Areas*.

The shoreline pattern of these harbours was modified by the effect of a renowned climatic event referred to as "the groundhog day storm." This storm devastated the harbours throughout Digby Neck and the Islands during the winter of 1976. It destroyed many wharves and processing facilities. Most marginal or already abandoned facilities were not rebuilt. Indeed, it could be argued that this storm speeded up the process of reducing the numbers of those engaged in the fisheries.

The Development of the Digby Neck and the Islands Economy

Digby Neck was settled primarily by English-speaking settlers from the United Kingdom and New England. Brier Island was first settled by a family from Maine in 1796. There were scattered settlements at Sandy Cove and on Long Island as well. However, it was not until the coming of the Empire Loyalists after 1783 that the contemporary pattern of settlement was completed (Deveau 1977: 55, 66–75). With the returned Acadians, who settled the area after the mid 1700s expulsion, these two populations laid the foundations for the area's present communities.

For most of the 19th century the traditional pattern of local marine resources exploitation was based upon family labour in the catching and curing of cod and pollock for the market, largely in the West Indies (Deveau 1977:93–99). A second tradition, particularly noticeable on Digby Neck, was the Grand Banks pattern:

> Handlining fishermen would work from small dories spreading out from a mother schooner, which would often stay on the fishing grounds for a week or even several weeks before returning to port. Life in the fishing villages was then geared to such absences of husbands and fathers (Hughes *et al.* 1960:50).

The modern fishery began to take shape after the introduction of gasoline engines at the turn of this century. This was followed by the adoption of open motor boats and, ultimately, by the Cape Island Boat which dominated the fishery until the recent development of the small dragger. It is still the main type of vessel for the coastal zone fleet, particularly the lobster fleet:

> This craft marked the beginning of a new era in the whole fishing industry of Saint Mary's Bay. The fisherman could go farther out and capture more fish. He could no longer afford the time ashore to cure and dry his fish. It was more profitable for him to concentrate on catching the fish and selling it to fish buyers, with salaried employees who became experts at cutting, curing, and preparing this fish for market. These fish buyers were, for the most part, former fishermen from the community. Usually they also set

up a store from which the fishermen would buy not only their fishing gear but also all their household needs (Deveau 1977:170).

World War II further transformed the industry and brought it out of the crisis of the depression years:

> Prosperity returned to the industry during the Second World War. The fish plants were enlarged, mechanization was introduced, and production streamlined. Many smaller operators could not adapt to the new methods and went out of business, allowing concentration of fish processing in a few ports and at the hands of a limited number of operators (Hughes *et al.* 1960:51–52).

Despite these trends, fish processing on Digby Neck is still largely in the hands of locally based processors, usually family firms.

The development of the Cape Island Boat made it possible to carry on the fishery as a local occupation. A pattern of day trips developed which was to characterise this fishery until the growth of the dragger fleet in the years after World War II. The Sterling County study carried out in the 1950s when the impact of this new technology was first being felt gives an idea of the response at that time (Hughes *et al.* 1960).

From the first there was concern about the long-term consequences of dragging, particularly as most local fishers had not initially adopted this technology. It was felt that local fishers would be unable to compete and that, in addition to its deleterious effect on stocks, dragging would challenge the continued viability of the fishing communities of the Neck and Islands (Hughes *et al.* 1960).

The authors of the Sterling County study supported this view by citing such factors as the development of individualism, which made necessary co-operation difficult and thus limited the possibility of adopting the new technology. In addition they proposed that economic reasons might see the new dragger fleet operating out of cities and towns closer to markets and fishing grounds.[2]

As is demonstrated below, these inhibitions and constraints did not last very long. The dragger technology was adopted with a vengeance. Although the communities did not become obsolete as predicted, many of the problems raised in the above passages are still relevant today.

In addition to the technological changes mentioned, a further series of changes have influenced these communities. For instance, the development of the welfare state has resulted in an ever growing involvement of the state in many aspects of community life.

Changes in access to the "outside" would have changed patterns of interaction as well. The Islands traditionally had links to the mainland via the Acadian shore of St. Mary's Bay. It was here that boats were built and purchased, as they still are. Today an improved road network and a provincially subsidized ferry service have led to a reorientation of the Islands communities in the direction of the commercial, medical and government facilities found in the town of Digby.

In addition, the 1981 Census Canada figures on the age and sex distribution of the area attest to the probability of future problems for these communities. When we compare the contemporary population distribution to the bell shaped distribution of Digby County in 1951 we see that the Digby Neck and Islands communities now show a flat distribution. Today there are more people in the older age groups and fewer in the economically active age groups, that is, those between 20 and 64. If patterns of substantial outmigration by young people prevail, as they have in the past, it is safe to predict that the distortions already present in the age structure of the population will be exaggerated in the future. Thus the viability question raised in the 1950s Sterling County study may become a serious problem (Hughes *et al.* 1960).

POPULATION AND EMPLOYMENT

Despite the fact that the population of Digby Neck has remained fairly constant between 1961 and 1981, the interval variation in these figures demonstrates meaningful changes. As Table 1 shows, the 5.2 percent overall increase for all of the communities masks some significant contrasts. The 22.8 percent growth of Centreville-Sandy Cove is best explained by: (1) the influence of proximity to Digby Town making commuting for work possible, (2) the growth of a summer tourist industry in Sandy Cove, and (3) its attractiveness as a place of residence for retired people. The large (16.3 percent) decline in Tiverton is largely explained by the decline in employment in the fishery and a shift of some services to Freeport. Freeport has become a service center for the Island communities, containing the consolidated high school and a home for the elderly, as well as the medical clinic and home of the local doctor, a bank and other services. Workers in processing jobs on both sides of Grand Passage also live in Freeport. The small decline in Westport represents the compensatory growth of fish processing which has served to buffer it from the decline in the ground-fishery. Finally, the increase shown by Little River-East Ferry reflects their importance as centers of the small dragger fishery and fish processing. Even more diagnostic than the overall population trends are the occupational profiles of these communities (see Appendix). Almost 60 percent of the labour force of 855 is employed in two sectors: 26.9 percent in fishing and trapping and 28.6 percent in manufacturing industries. The latter can be interpreted as fish processing since this is the only manufacturing industry on Digby Neck and the Islands. Thus the employment profile of these communities is characteristic of single-sector communities. All of the other occupations are concerned with the provision of services to the fishery, either directly, or indirectly, by providing support to families which are in turn, supported by the fisheries. The exception to this pattern is the large proportion of jobs in the community business and personal service industries located in Freeport. As mentioned above, this reflects Freeport's development as a service centre for the Island.

TABLE 1: Population by Place for Digby Neck and the Islands Community Areas 1966, 1971, 1981

Community Areas	Year 1966 N	1971 N	1981 N	% Change 1966–1971	1971–1981	1966–1981
Centreville-Sandy Cove	452	436	555	-3.5	+27.3	+22.8
Little River-East Ferry	428	439	450	+2.6	+2.5	+5.1
Tiverton	454	371	380	-18.3	+2.4	-16.3
Freeport	395	475	465	+20.3	-2.1	+17.7
Westport	367	380	355	+3.5	-6.6	-3.3
TOTAL	2096	2101	2205	+0.2	+5.0	+5.2

Sources: J. A. Deveau, *Along the Shores of St. Mary's Bay*, Vol. 1, 1977 for 1966, 1971, and Statistics Canada, Census for 1981.

Employment in the fishing related sectors is predominantly male (98.8 percent). In processing, males also dominate numerically, accounting for 63.3 percent of all positions. Processing sector employment is characterised by great seasonal variation. Yet, a much higher percentage of permanent employees are males. Women are usually hired to do specific types of processing tasks such as packing fish, while men are employed in a wider range of tasks such as cutting, splitting, salting and so on.

Fishers show a similar fluctuation in employment on a seasonal basis. This fluctuation is, in large part, influenced by the impact of weather and government regulations on access to stocks. Many participate in the groundfish dragger fishery and the small boat lobster fishery, and also depend on unemployment insurance to balance the round of yearly activities.

The fact that all of these communities have one or more fish plants or are close to fish plants needing labour is reflected in the predominance of processing sector employment. Since labour is most frequently drawn from the communities within which the plants are located, plant owners and managers are usually personally familiar with their employees, employees' families and the like. Indeed, the personal substance of plant owner/manager—employee relations constitutes a meaningful social dimension in workplace and employment dynamics. These relations colour the employment practices of plant owners and set the context for the socio-economic connectedness of fish plants to particular communities. For instance, plant owners reported that they felt obligated to offer the first opportunity of employment to people from the surrounding community. Conversely, local people with bad reputations can be denied access to employment.

In sum, the settlement and development of Digby Neck and the Islands were conditioned largely by the region's proximity to one of the most bountiful ocean resource environments in Atlantic Canada. From the outset, the people, their industry and their communities have been fisheries dependent and thoroughly integrated within the Northeastern Seaboard, fisheries-levered, socio-economic systems. The situation has remained to this day. Indeed, the decline of household-based production of food and other goods, largely for self-consumption, has led to an even greater dependency upon the fisheries. Few now have the ability to fall back on household resources for subsistence in this age of reliance on store-bought goods and services. In short, the vitality of the fisheries has become even more essential to the region's present prosperity and future development. The dilemmas resulting from this circumstance, particularly as a consequence of recent changes in the structure and dynamic of the fisheries, will become vividly apparent in the description and analysis which follows.

A Profile of the Fishing Industry   **3**

"Around here ya either fish, work with fish or hang around and throw rocks at gulls. That's all there is." This statement by a Centreville fisher accurately expresses the dependence of the people of Digby Neck and the Islands on the fishing industry for their livelihood. It's an historical dependence that has intensified with time. Agriculture, lumbering and farming are no longer even supplementary economic pursuits to the fisheries. Consequently, the organisation and characteristics of the fishing industry influences the annual cycle of social and economic activities in Digby Neck and the Islands communities. This is most dramatically illustrated by the ways in which changes in the industry have affected communities and livelihoods.

As has occurred throughout southwest Nova Scotia, technological change in the fisheries and the concomitant transformation of the production and processing of marine resources have fundamentally reshaped much of the fishing industry in the Digby Neck and the Islands area. This has been particularly the case since the late 1940s.

FISH PRODUCTION

Throughout the 20th century, the southwest Nova Scotia small boat fishery has been dominated by one type of boat — the Cape Islander, named after its place of origin, Cape Sable Island, Shelburne County (see Figure 1). A very seaworthy, shallow draft vessel, the Cape Island design provides fishers with a motorised boat offering a large working platform stretching from the foresection to the stern. It was originally built of locally available wood and was relatively inexpensive. Today the hull design can be found in a wide variety of vessel sizes and construction materials. Many of the new Cape Islanders seen tied to Digby Neck wharves are built of fiberglass and are wider and longer than their predecessors. Most contemporary small boats

Figure 1: The Cape Island Boat

Source: Reprinted with permission from L.B. Jenson, Fishermen of Nova Scotia. Halifax: Petheric Press Limited, 1980.

are outfitted with a number of electronic and mechanical aids—echo sounders, radar, marine radios, motor driven hoists, citizens' band radios and loran bearing/location units. Much of this is a recent addition to small boat fishing, augmenting and, in some instances, replacing traditional fishing devices such as sounding leads, mental calculation of compass direction and steering time, and local knowledge of the fishing grounds. Indeed, the adaptation of these devices in the small boat fishery has dramatically affected the role of experience, in so far as electronic aids reduce the need for prospective captains to undergo extensive crew apprenticeships. Surrounded by an array of instruments, individuals are now able to step aboard a boat as captains with relatively little experience.

The Digby Neck and the Islands fishers mainly use Cape-Island type boats within the coastal zones adjacent to their home ports (see Map 4). To fishers the marine environment is a complex system composed of specific places where resources either can or cannot be exploited. Often parts of the ocean environment are named by local fishers. Many names, such as "the Pinnacle," "the Rip," "the Deep Hole" and "Head and Horns," simply describe the environment's physical features. Other names such as "Sandy Cove Ground" and "Whale Cove Ground" are derived from their proximity to specific harbours. A few spots are named after the individual who discovered the place, while others reflect the onshore mark used as a location reference point.[1] Every name conjures up precise images in the fishers' mind concerning the topographical features of the ocean bottom, the water depth, location from port, availability of specific types of resources, accessibility at certain times of the year in specific weather conditions, and the biological profile of the ocean floor. Images and knowledge of this sort are fundamental to fishers striving to extract their livelihoods from coastal zones. It provides them with an experientially-grounded information base from which they can develop daily and seasonal fishing strategies.

Fishers from the different harbours frequently exploit a portion of the coastal resource zone which they consider "our fishin' ground." That is, the persons fishing out of each harbour claim rights of first access to resources located within commonly defined portions of the coastal marine environment. The portions claimed represent those areas that have been exploited continually by generations of fishers working out of each harbour. As such, this arrangement amounts to a property claim based upon decades of use. Every harbour's fishers know and generally respect the boundaries that separate their grounds from those of persons fishing out of the neighbouring harbours. These conditions are particularly

Map 4: Coastal Zone Fishing Grounds

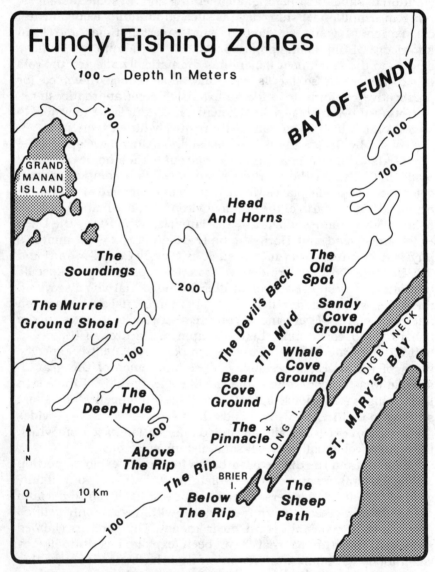

Fundy Fishing Zones

100 Depth In Meters

BAY OF FUNDY

100

100

100

GRAND
MANAN
ISLAND

Head
And Horns

The Soundings

The
Old
Spot

The Murre
Ground Shoal

200

The Devil's Back

The Mud

Sandy
Cove
Ground

100

Whale
Cove
Ground

DIGBY NECK

The
Deep Hole

Bear
Cove
Ground

200

N

The
Pinnacle

×

LONG I.

ST. MARY'S BAY

Above
The Rip

0   10 Km

The Rip

BRIER
I.

Below
The Rip

The
Sheep
Path

100

Cartographer: Austin Rodgers

important in the high value lobster fishery. An older Tiverton fisher described the situation in this manner:

> We always fished lobster on ground to the sou'west in St. Mary's Bay and the Bay of Fundy. All along these shores of Long Island. Men from East Ferry go lobsterin' along the nor'east side of the Neck. Westporters fish down below and all around Briar Island while Freeporters lobster up the nor'est sides of Long Island. We all know where we lobster and look out if ya edge into the other fella's grounds.

Harbour-focused property claims, while most important in the lobster fishery, also exist in the groundfish and herring fisheries. This is particularly the case for fixed gear types of fishing such as longline, herring net and herring weir activity. In these fisheries the boundaries are more flexible than those associated with the lobster fishery. Often they are simply defined in terms of the geographical area that can be exploited effectively by persons working in a day fishery. For instance, coastal zone fishers from Tiverton cannot exploit the groundfish resources situated below Briar Island as economically as those working out of Westport. Westporters are more closer to these grounds, and therefore better able to reach them every fishing day. The same limits apply on Westport fishing efforts in grounds commonly exploited by fishers from Tiverton. However, fishers from neighbouring harbours such as Westport/Freeport and Tiverton/East Ferry often exploit the same grounds. So, property claims in the groundfish and herring fisheries are expressed more generally, and reflect the similarity of interests, activities and limitations shared by neighbouring harbours.[2] As is shown below, the organisation and access management effects of these property relation systems were disrupted by two developments: the introduction of mobile, high production fishing technologies such as drag net fishing and herring seining, and federal government regulatory measures such as limited entry licences and quotas.

The coastal zone fishery encompasses a variety of resource production activities, the major ones being lobster fishing, hook and line groundfishing, herring gill net fishing, weir fishing and some fish dragging (see Figure 2). The coastal zone fishery is seasonal in that fishers pursue specific resources at different times of the year. Lobster fishing is the only activity with a formally defined season. Government regulations specify that non-berried (egg carrying) lobsters with a minimum carapace length of 3 and 3/16 inches can be caught and sold only between the last Monday of November and the first of June by licensed fishers in District 4A, the district within which Digby Neck and the Islands are located. Most full-time and

Figure 2: Coastal Zone Fishing Technologies

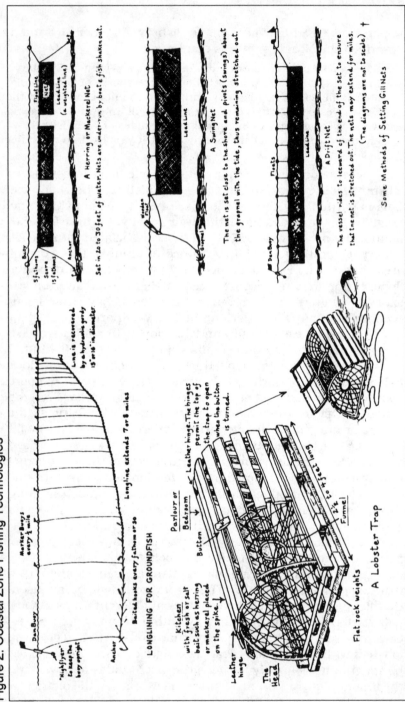

A Herring or Mackerel Net

Set in 20 to 30 feet of water. Nets are under-run by boat & fish shaken out.

A Swing Net

The net is set close to the shore and pivots (swings) about the grapnel with the tide, thus remaining stretched out.

A Drift Net

The vessel rides to leeward of the end of the set to ensure that the net is stretched out. The nets may extend for miles.

(The diagrams are not to scale.) †

Some Methods of Setting Gill Nets

LONGLINING FOR GROUNDFISH

Longline extends 7 or 8 miles

Line is recovered by a hydraulic gurdy 15" wide in diameter.

Marker Buoys every ¼ mile

Baited hooks every fathom or so

"High flyers" to keep the buoy upright

Dan Buoy

Anchor

Kitchen with fresh or salt bait such as herring or mackerel placed on the spike.

Leather hinge

A Lobster Trap

The Head

Parlour or Bedroom

Button

Leather hinge. The hinges permit the top of the trap to open when the button is turned.

3 to 4 feet long

1½ Funnel

Flat rock weights

Source: Reprinted with permission from L.B. Jenson, *Fishermen of Nova Scotia*. Halifax: Petheric Press Limited, 1980.

part-time fishers participate in this fishery, some fishing throughout the winter months. All other fisheries are pursued when the particular species are most available. For instance, the fishers use gill nets to catch herring when the fish is "runnin'." They switch to hook and line fishing when stocks of cod, haddock and pollock "come on the ground." It is common for coastal zone fishers to switch fishing gears and fishing strategies throughout the season.

An outstanding feature of the Cape Island Boat is the ease with which it can be adapted to a variety of types of fishing. As Figure 2 shows, it can be used for handline and long line baited hook fishing. In addition, it is relatively easy to change gear for the lobster season and, formerly, Cape Island Boats were rigged seasonally for the herring. Currently, most of these boats are utilised primarily in the lobster fishery and/or for handlining. This type of vessel is used mainly for daily trips to fishing grounds.

The nature of the hook and line technology, with its high degree of selectivity, is such that it largely captures mature fish, leaving juveniles for further growth. That is, fisher manipulations of both baits, such as fresh herring, frozen mackerel and frozen squid, and hook sizes, for example smaller hook 'fine gear' or larger cod hooks, permits them to select successfully for desired species and fish sizes. Moreover, since it is a technology which lies on the ocean floor, it only minimally disturbs the spawning and feeding of young fish on the bottom. In these ecological and environmental characteristics, it contrasts markedly with dragger technology.

Crew size on Cape Island Boats is small, one to two per vessel. Most boats are owned and crewed by immediate kin or familiars. Father-son configurations are common. A division of labour such as that within the coastal zone fishery is largely undeveloped. Captain and crew generally participate more or less equally in all work tasks, but it's the captain's prerogative to make decisions concerning where to fish and the pace of work. However, crews commonly discuss fishing strategies with their captains and also influence the organisation and pace of work. For instance, the crew may stop fishing for a drink or a bite to eat, after providing the captain with little more than notification of the pending work interruption.

During handline fishing, each fisher occupies a station on the platform where he works his own lines, with the captain most commonly fishing adjacent to the boat's wheel and instrumentation. So, each fisher has virtual autonomy over the pace and character of his labour, able to work or rest at discretion without interrupting the labour processes of the other. Longlining demands much more co-ordination within the labour process, particularly during setting

and hauling back the gear. Captain and crew work as one, sys-
tematically feeding ("shooting") the baited tubs of line over the boat's
stern. Usually longline sets occur very rapidly as the forward motion
of the boat "shoots" the anchored and buoy-marked line over the
stern, often out of a wood or metal device referred to as a "trawl
shoot." Tubs of line are interconnected, marked with buoy ropes and
fed out by the crew while the captain steers the boat, determines the
speed of the set and monitors direction and location through observations of radar and echo-sounder readings. When the line is being
hauled back the captain and crew often take turns at the primary
tasks. While one is "tendin' the rail," (removing fish and old bait from
hooks as the line is pulled over a steel roller attached to the side of
the boat adjacent to the wheel), the other sits on a box behind the
hydraulic hoist and coils the longline back into its tubs. Once one
or the other tires of their task, they arrange to switch off. Of course,
individual discretion over the longlining labour process is much
more circumscribed than is that associated with handline fishing.
The necessary co-ordination of tasks means that the entire process
of work is interrupted when any one person takes a break, a
circumstance which gives longline fishing a more formal character
than that associated with handline fishing. Similar co-ordination of
captain-crew activity is integral to lobster and gill net fishing labour
processes. Yet, the entire coastal zone fishery labour process is
contextualised by social familiarity, if not outright kin-relatedness,
countering the development of a division of labour that entrenches
formal social divisions between fishers. A fundamental "we're all in
the same boat" sentiment pervades relations and work.

The relatively low purchase and operating costs of Cape Island
boats meant that in the past a large number of these boats were
locally owned and gave employment to a great number of persons.
All fishers could reasonably aspire to owning a boat sometime in
their working lives. Thus, small boat fishing harbours were ordinarily hives of activity, with many vessels coming in, going out, or riding
at anchor on any day.

In addition to the Cape Island Boat, numerous small draggers,
between 45 and 65 feet in length are used in the Digby Neck and the
Islands fisheries (see Figure 3). These vessels are equipped as stern
trawlers, using otter trawl technology to catch groundfish (see
Figure 4). The otter trawl, a bag-net fishing technology, is towed
behind the fishing boat. "Trawl doors," located between the "warp"
and "cable," are designed and attached so that the force of the tow
against them keeps the net spread. The mouth of the net is kept
open during the tow by "headline floats." Various types of rollers

Figure 3: The Small Boat Dragger

Source: Reprinted with permission from L.B. Jenson, *Fishermen of Nova Scotia*. Halifax: Petheric Press Limited, 1980.

Figure 4: The Otter Trawl

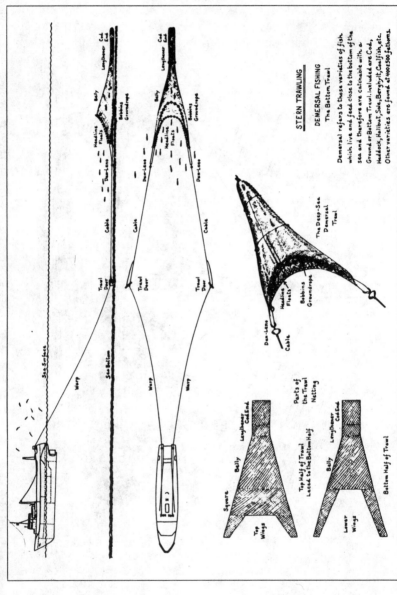

STERN TRAWLING

DEMERSAL FISHING
The Bottom Trawl

Demersal refers to those varieties of fish which live and feed close to the bottom of the sea and therefore are catchable with a Ground or Bottom Trawl. Included are Cod, Haddock, Halibut, Sole, Bergylt, Catfish, etc. Other varieties are found at 400 to 500 fathoms.

Source: Reprinted with permission from L.B. Jenson, *Fishermen of Nova Scotia*. Halifax: Petheric Press Limited, 1980.

arranged on a steel cable "ground line" guide the net over the ocean bottom. Since it is towed through the water, the otter trawl is classified as a mobile fishing gear. Many captains employ a variety of electronic aids to locate fish. Once concentrations are identified (schools or shoals) the net is set over the boat's stern at a depth necessary to capture the fish. The captain then tows the net through the water at a speed that allows the boat to overtake and pass through the shoal. In this fishery, the division of labour is formal, and the labour process is fragmented, reflecting a command structure.

A crew size of two to five is usual on the Cape St. Mary's-type fish dragger. Most boats have three persons on board, the captain and two crew (also referred to as winchmen). The captain decides where to fish, when to set the net, when to haul the net and the length of the trip. Winchmen do most of the manual work. They stand behind the cable winches during sets and haulbacks, guiding the cable either off of or onto the rollers. They also perform tasks such as setting the trawl doors, dumping the net, sorting and icing the catch, and mending tears in the net mesh. In these boats the captains hold the position of total command. The crew quickly follow the captain's directions and do not hesitate, when in doubt, to ask him what they should do.

The drag net is towed through the water for as little as one-half hour up to more than three hours at a time. The duration depends upon the captain's expectations. While the net is in the water captain and crew do little but stand watch, monitor the instrument readings, eat, talk and rest. When the captain signals they are to begin hauling back, the boat becomes alive with activity. Every haulback is awaited with high anticipation, almost excitement. The size and the species composition of the catch are extremely important to these commercial fishers. The trawl doors breaking water signal that the net is not far behind. All eyes gaze over the stern looking for the cod end and indications that the tow was a good one. Promising signs heighten the anticipation and seem to fuel the pace of work. With discouraging signs the crew turns away from the stern and begins the seemingly yeoman task of hauling it into the boat. Most of these boats will stay out until the captain is either satisfied with the catch or convinced further effort would only waste time and money. Trips are frequently between two and five days long, depending on the time of year and the grounds being fished.

Otter trawls fished by 45 to 65 foot boats have proven to be the most cost efficient and productive operation in the Nova Scotian fishing industry.[3] This method can produce more fish, faster and more economically, than any other type of fishing technology, whether coastal zone hook and line or large vessel trawler. Small draggers have high volume catches and fast turnaround times between the fishing grounds and the landing port. Consequently, in order to return full benefits to their operators these boats must exploit large stocks situated close to a landing port. Conditions requiring captains to travel great distances in search of fish quickly erode the basis of small dragger economic efficiency. Digby Neck is at a disadvantage compared to other areas with regard to access to the more distant and rich banks of southwest Nova Scotia (see Map 5). First priority is given to the exploitation of banks in the Bay of Fundy and St. Mary's Bay area. However, declining stocks have made it necessary to exploit more distant banks. The costs in fuel and time have led some of the vessels to land their fish at ports closer to these banks. Many captains occasionally tie their vessels up in these ports and have the crews commute to and from Digby Neck and the Islands by car. A number of draggers spend part of the year at ports such as Meteghan and Shelburne, although they are owned and crewed by fishers from Digby Neck and the Islands.

There have been many compositional changes in the Digby Neck and the Islands fishing fleet over the years. Table 2 clearly illustrates some of the broad characteristics of these changes between 1953 and 1972. These data show a marked increase in larger sized vessels over 10 tons, from 43 in 1953 to 59 in 1972. Even more dramatic is the fourfold growth in the otter trawler fleet, from no boats in 1953–1954 to 28 in 1970. Conversely, while the total number of boats under 10 tons remained relatively stable between 1953 and 1972, the portion of the fleet composed of boats under 30 feet in length declined by almost 50 percent. These data reveal that the Digby Neck and the Islands fleet underwent a notable change during this period. By 1970 the fleet was composed of much larger vessels with a greater capacity to catch fish.

Between 1970 and 1983 the fleet underwent a further significant reorganisation, as is evident in a comparison of data profiled in Tables 2 and 3. As can be seen in Table 3, the coastal zone sector, between 1979–1983, experienced a decrease of 23.3 percent in boats categorised in the range of 30 to 40 feet or greater in length. Notably, the under 30 feet category has shown an increase in numbers of boats, from 13 in 1979 to 25 or more by 1983. This switch in the fleet's small boat component reflects an important decline in the full-time coastal zone fishery and an associated rise in a seasonal lobster fishing specialisation. Only small boats are required to fish lobster. The decline in the inshore fleet has been balanced by an

Map 5: Offshore Fishing Grounds

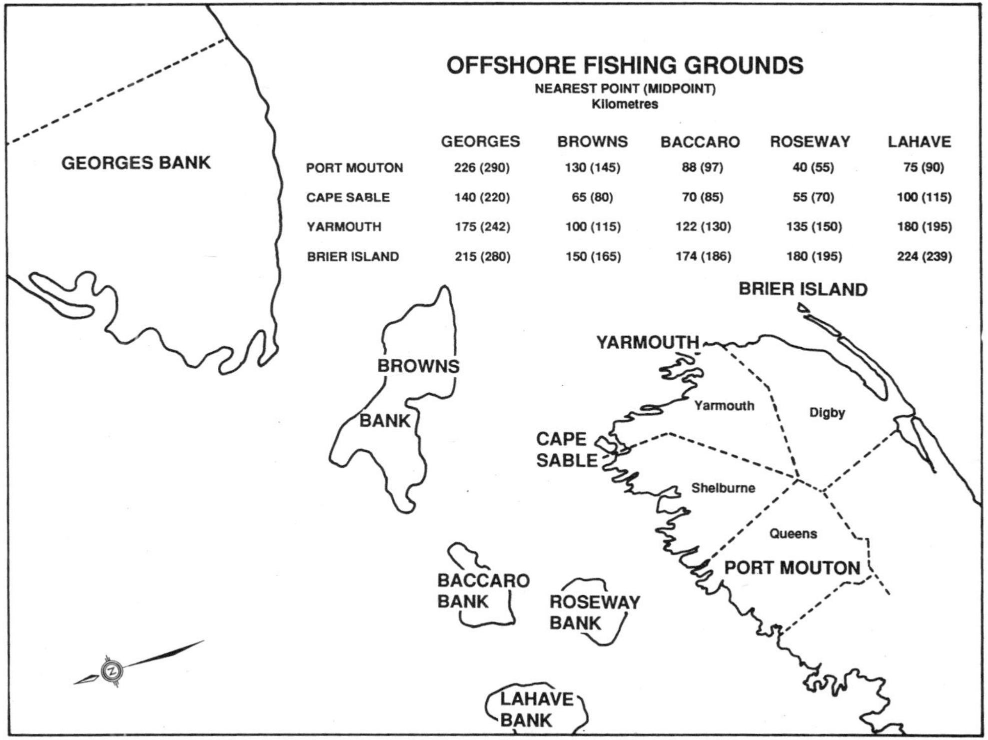

OFFSHORE FISHING GROUNDS
NEAREST POINT (MIDPOINT)
Kilometres

	GEORGES	BROWNS	BACCARO	ROSEWAY	LAHAVE
PORT MOUTON	226 (290)	130 (145)	88 (97)	40 (55)	75 (90)
CAPE SABLE	140 (220)	65 (80)	70 (85)	55 (70)	100 (115)
YARMOUTH	175 (242)	100 (115)	122 (130)	135 (150)	180 (195)
BRIER ISLAND	215 (280)	150 (165)	174 (186)	180 (195)	224 (239)

Source: Anthony Davis, A.J. Hanson, L. Kasdan and R. Apostle. *Utilization of Offshore Banks by the Small Boat Fisheries in Southwest Nova Scotia*.

TABLE 2: Motorised Boats. <10 Tons and >10 Tons. Digby Neck and the Islands (District 37), 1953–1972

		Motorised Boats		
		<10 tons		>10 tons
Year	(N)	< 30 ft. in length	(N)	Otter Trawlers
1953	151	N/A	43	-
1954	151	N/A	45	-
1955	140	N/A	39	7
1956	125	N/A	52	10
1957	133	N/A	44	10
1961	154	35	42	13
1962	159	34	50	16
1963	167	38	48	19
1964	160	38	55	23
1965	174	56	64	25
1966	156	29	59	22
1967	156	29	59	22
1968	158	28	60	22
1969	157	27	62	23
1970	156	21	63	28
1972	146	18	59	-

Source: Department of Fisheries and Oceans.

TABLE 3: Motorised Boats by Length and Sector (Coastal Zone/Offshore), Digby Neck and the Islands (District 37), 1979–1983

	Coastal Zone				Offshore			
	Boat Length (feet)				Boat Length (feet)			
Year	<30	30–34	35–39	40>	<45	45–64	65>	Total
1979	13	25	73	18	2	15	9	155
1980	16	24	77	20	6	23	7	173
1981	31	17	67	21	14	21	-	171
1982	27	18	63	22	16	23	-	169
1983	25	20	58	11	17	21	-	152

Source: Department of Fisheries and Oceans, Statistical Branch.

eightfold increase in the number of boats falling in the less than 45 feet category and a 43 percent increase in those in the 45–64 feet category. Here we see the continued growth of the offshore sector, especially the dragger component of the fleet. These processes reveal the extent to which the Digby Neck and Islands fisheries have changed in recent years.

As might be anticipated, changes in the composition of the fishing fleet are associated with similar changes in the extent of employment in fish production. Table 4 profiles the number of boats and fishers engaged in the Digby Neck and Islands fisheries between 1953 and 1983. These data reveal rather dramatic declines in the number of fishers and fishing boats, a 31.9 percent decline in the former and a 51.5 percent decline in the latter. Thus, even though the average number of fishers per boat increased from 1.4 to 1.9, this was not enough to absorb the fishers displaced by the decline in total number of boats. In other words, though the dragger portion of the fleet experienced significant growth during the years profiled, the mechanised character of this fishing effort kept the increase in crew size to a minimum. Consequently, growth in the dragger fleet did not provide employment opportunities for those displaced from the coastal zone fisheries, nor did it sustain previous levels of employment. The overall pattern has been movement towards greater catch capacity combined with an increased mechanisation that results in reductions in overall employment.

Fish Processing

The drastic changes which took place in the fishing sector were paralleled by equally sweeping changes in fish processing. In the past, this sector was labour intensive with low capital costs. Start up costs for processors were low; a wooden building, wooden work benches, wooden boxes, a source of water and refrigeration were the major requirements for a processing plant. This accounts for the great number of small plants in the area in the past (e.g., 28 in 1962). This also explains why a cycle of entrance, success or failure, and succession was a common feature of the processing sector in these communities. Most of the entrepreneurs were locals who had spent time in the fisheries. These plants depended on labour normally drawn from the local community. In addition, the mix of processes and products up until the mid 1960s was quite different from what is found today. Salted and dried and smoked fish were dominant features of the economy, supplemented by fish oil extraction and some canning. Salting in particular was quite labour intensive and could involve children as well as women. In some cases, fishing families operated as an enterprise which sold the finished product to locally based middlemen who moved the product to various markets.

At present there are far fewer plants on Digby Neck than there were in the past. The distribution is as follows: Westport 1, Tiverton 1, East Ferry 3, Tiddville 1, Little River 2, Mink Cove 1 (a fishmeal reduction plant), Lake Midway 2, and Centreville 1. This decrease from 28 in 1962 to 12 in 1985 reflects the greatly increased capital costs associated with entry as well as other structural changes within the industry which will be discussed below.

TABLE 4: Number of Fishermen, Number of Boats. Average Number of Fishermen Per Boat, Digby Neck and the Islands (District 37), Selected Years Between 1953–1983.

Year	Fishermen N	% Change Annual	Boats N	% Change Annual	Average No. of Fishermen Per Boat
1953	539	-	396	-	1.4
1954	551	+2.2	399	+1.0	1.4
1955	638	+15.8	389	-2.5	1.6
1956	627	-1.7	364	-6.4	1.7
1957[1]	550	-12.3	201	-44.8	2.7
1961	368	-33.1	237	+17.9	1.6
1963	383	+4.1	247	+4.2	1.6
1965	425	+11.0	243	-1.6	1.8
1967	409	-3.8	225	-7.4	1.8
1969	398	-2.7	222	-1.3	1.8
1970	386	-3.0	221	-0.5	1.8
1972	400	+3.6	205	-7.2	2.0
1978	N/A	-	201	-2.0	N/A
1979	N/A	-	196	-2.5	N/A
1980	329	-17.8	215	+9.7	1.5
1981	333	+1.2	202	-6.1	1.7
1982	328	-1.5	187	-7.4	1.8
1983	367	-11.9	192	+2.7	1.9
% change 1953–1983	-	-31.9	-	51.5	-

Source: Department of Fisheries and Oceans, Statistical Branch.

1. During this year the number of boats classified as "other" (rowboats, smacks, etc.) totalled 14, while in the previous year 177 boats were thus classified.

Seven owners/managers of contemporary Digby Neck and the Islands fish plants agreed to participate in lengthy, formal interviews concerning various aspects of their business. These owners/managers operated fish plants that range in the value of capital equipment from $125,000 through $500,000 to $1.6 million, with 1984 fish sales ranging in value from $1 million through $4 million to $6 million. In other words, a variety of small, medium and large scale fish plant enterprises are represented in the owner/manager interviews.

All of the owners/managers interviewed were born and raised in Digby Neck and the Islands communities, most frequently in the actual community within which their fish plant is located. Four of the seven interviewed inherited their position and the fish plant from their fathers, while the remaining three began their careers as fishers. As fishers they all had tremendously successful careers as owners and operators of small boat fish draggers, starting their fish plants up, in part, with the wealth they had generated from this fishery. In addition, most of the owners/managers interviewed reported that many members of their immediate families as well as those of their wives' participate in the fishing industry. All of the owners/managers interviewed are people, in practically every way imaginable, "of" Digby Neck and the Islands communities, with a personal background of thorough integration in and experience with the fishing industry.

Notably, none of these people, whether or not the recipients of extensive school education, reported receiving any specific formal training in business management development and/or needs of owning and operating a fish processing enterprise. They all claimed that their business acumen, and marketing strategies were, and continue to be, largely the expression of personal experience within the industry. The owners/managers with a family history of fish plant ownership describe their experience as developed within networks of established business practices and contacts. For instance, marketing was reported most often as a continuation of practices developed and employed by the current owners'/managers' fathers. In contrast, the owners/managers who began as fishers claim to have developed markets through a simple expression of personal initiative in establishing contacts and building marketing relationships of reliability, confidence and mutual satisfaction, that is, through positive reputation. A couple of these even noted that several owners of established fish firms, supposed competitors, provided very helpful advice and initial contacts. So, experience, whether acquired in the context of established networks or through entrepreneurial initiatives, constitutes the background and the substance of business practices for Digby Neck and the Islands fish plant owners/managers. Of course, there are qualities that underwrite the perception of fish processing as a manufacturing industry built upon, some would say mired in, traditional ways of doing things. The fish plant owners'/managers' low opinion of the role of formal education in their business lends further support to the notion that tradition and entrepreneurial initiative rule in these enterprises.

At present plants differ in appearance from those of the past. Government sanitary regulations, market demand and adoption of mechanised processing technologies have increased the capitalisation of plants substantially. These, in turn, have resulted in changes in some aspects of the labour processes such as task specialisation, fragmentation of work, and reduced labour inputs per unit of product. Oil extraction and canning have completely disappeared. Today fresh and frozen fillets are the dominant products, while a smaller amount of salted and smoked fish is still processed. Production takes place in plants with poured concrete floors and stainless steel benches and tables. Skinning and filleting machines, flash freezing and ice making machinery, conveyer belts, fork lift trucks, plastic tubs and the like are common components in the contemporary Digby Neck and the Islands fish plants.

Given these changes, it is not surprising that entrance into processing is more difficult than in the past. Continuous operation is a must in order to make a profit. Continuity of supply is potentially much more of a concern to the contemporary plant owner/manager than it was in the past. Two strategies have been developed to address this concern: (1) processor ownership (full or as partners) in the dragger fleet, and (2) trucking supply in from other plants when not enough is available locally. These trends receive fuller attention later in the study.

Interviews with the owners/managers of seven Digby Neck and the Islands fish plants reveal several important features concerning the organisation and characteristics of fish plant work. Five of these plants were reported to employ between 20 and 60 persons while the remaining two each provided paid work for well over 100 persons. While quite diverse in scale, the work forces in all of the plants exhibit similar characteristics and experience similar circumstances. All of the plant owners/managers reported varying degrees of seasonality in their business operations. While most are open for business over the entire year, the April to November peak season in fish landings generates work for well over 480 persons, most of them locals. The December through March low season commonly finds the work force reduced by 50 percent, sometimes as much as 90 percent. Inclement and unpredictable winter weather keeps the fishing boats in port, making fish landings uncertain and resource supply scarce. Indeed, several of the plant owners/ managers reported that their businesses are only kept open through the practice of trucking fish in from places such as Cape Breton and Newfoundland. Most of the unemployed workers qualify for and draw unemployment insurance benefits (U.I.) throughout the low season.

While the vast majority of plant workers are "called in" only when needed to process available supply, high and relatively stable levels of resource landings throughout the peak season ordinarily provide full-time employment for the work force, often including overtime work. However, throughout the low season many fish plant workers would be fortunate to obtain an average of one day's work for every week. Consequently, obtaining sufficient weeks of work to qualify for unemployment insurance benefits is a key objective for many, although the length of the peak season assures most that sufficient employment will be available. Only one of the seven owners/ managers interviewed stated that he consciously "managed" employment in his plant "in order to make sure that any full-time employees got enough weeks in to qualify for U.I." Of course, the availability of employment in the fish plants as well as access to U.I. benefits are contingent upon the supply of marine resources, particularly groundfish.

Aside from its precarious qualities, employment income is also relatively low in Digby Neck and the Islands fish plants (see *Task Force on the Atlantic Fisheries* 1982:70 ff). The owners/managers interviewed reported that most of their employees earned between five and eight dollars per hour (83 percent of all employees). Indeed, all of the owners/managers reported similar wage scales, citing local competition for available labour as one of the primary factors influencing wage rates. Notably, six of the seven owners/managers claimed that greater than 75 percent of their workforces had been employed with them for over five years. Such employment stability suggests that factors other than wage rate competition exert substantial influences on labour market dynamics. For instance, most of the workers in the plants are local, drawn from surrounding communities and, as reported by the owners/managers, live within a ten-mile radius of the plant. Most communities have only one or two fish plants, and these provide the most significant private sector employment. As such, the outcome of limited intra- and inter-community competition for available labour provides existing plants with a virtual locational monopoly over employment and the labour market, a monopoly expressed in both the level and uniformity of reported wage rates.[4]

Across the board uniformities are evident in the location of men and women within fish plant wage scales. Women constitute 63 percent of all workers reported by owners/managers to be earning $5.99 per hour or less (142 of 227 workers) and fully 71 percent of all paid $4.99 or less per hour (48 of 60 employees). Conversely, men constitute 78 percent of workers reported to be earning $6.00 or more per hour (158 of 202) and over 86 percent of those paid $7.00 or more per hour (94 of 109). When specifically asked if they hired women for particular types of jobs, *all* of the owners/managers described hiring practices consistent with those of the owner who stated, "I hire women for packaging and weighing in the plant and book work in the office."

This practice is underlined by the distribution of men and women across fish plant job categories, as this was described by the owners/managers. Sixty-four percent of all females were reported employed as light labour: workers engaged in the lower paying jobs of trimming, candling, weighing, machine operating and packaging fish (almost 78 percent of all labour in this latter category). Moreover, only 28 percent of the more highly paid cutters and splitters are women and women make up fewer than 23 percent of those described as doing multiple jobs. Only 2 of 15 production line and plant floor supervisors are reported to be women.

In short, women workers are ghettoized in fish plants. They are predominant in the lower paying, less skilled production jobs. In contrast, men are more often situated in the skilled, higher paying jobs. Additionally, men are predominant in supervisory and technical jobs. Women, as a consequence of the fact that they are hired primarily for specific tasks, are subject to much greater employment insecurity than are men who are more commonly hired to work at a variety of tasks. The majority of women are hired after, and laid off before, most men.

None of the fish plant work force on Digby Neck and the Islands is organised into a collective bargaining body. All of the owners/managers interviewed reported intensely negative feelings about trade unions. As one stated, "We don't need unions here. They'd only upset everything. Most of the plants here take care of their employees, making work available when it is possible and making sure the work is spread around. Unions would make it hard on everybody." Aside from the rather predictable sentiments of owners/

managers, informal conversations with several male and female plant workers also indicate there would be little support for collective bargaining forms of organisation. Anti-union thinking and feelings are common throughout southwest Nova Scotia. In part, these reflect and are reinforced by particular social structural and psychological conditions in fisheries dependent communities.

Some of these conditions are a consequence of the systematic paternalistic patronage practised by the owners/managers. For instance, all but one of the owners/managers interviewed acknowledged that they commonly provide cash advances, credit and other forms of financial assistance for their full-time employees. Moreover, the owners/managers all said that they knew and pursued, within the parameters and abilities of their businesses, the best interests of "their" employees and communities. As one owner declared:

> Without my plant and business there would be widespread un-employment here. How my business goes is how employment goes. It's as simple as that. We do what we can to make work for the people, what our business will allow. We do our best to take care of them.

In addition, control of access to paid work allows owners/managers to exercise self-interested discretion over the terms and conditions of employment. All but one of the owners/managers interviewed identified the reputation of prospective employees as a factor second only to skill in hiring decisions. In small communities, such as those in Digby Neck and the Islands, the intimacies and public qualities of social life leave little room for second chances when one acquires a "negative" reputation. Of course, the constituent elements of the category "negative" are to some extent variable, depending on circumstances and situations. From the point of view of owners/managers, as reflected through the course of the interviews, persons known as lazy, tardy, unco-operative and troublesome ordinarily are blocked from obtaining paid work in Digby Neck and the Islands fish plants. Positive work habits and a co-operative disposition are valued, sought after, and cultivated employee qualities. To this end, one owner even noted that he "... pays a Christmas bonus to some workers. We determine who gets it by their work habits and co-operative behaviour."

Without question, the importance of fish plant employment in small fishing communities provides owners/managers with considerable discretionary power over the terms and conditions of work. These are social conditions under which none but the most courageous would attempt activities such as union organisation, petitions for improved wages and working conditions or any other activity that fish plant owners/managers could interpret as contrary to the interests of their businesses. The social conditions of work assure worker conformity to the terms and conditions set by owners/ managers, especially in circumstances where labour supply general- ly exceeds the availability of full-time work. These are conditions under which owners/managers are in a tremendously advantaged position, able to pursue the interests of their businesses through generally unfettered control of employment.

In such circumstances it is easy to envision draconian employ- ment practices. Many of those familiar only with the urban, industrial work world might take a hard view of the socio-economic and working conditions of fish plant employment. At the peak of summer production the smell, the frantic pace, the wet, the cold and the long hours of the fish plant work place might repel the uninitiated. Some could not imagine themselves working under those conditions; and would be shocked at the realisation that such work places even exist in contemporary, humane Canada. But, appearances do not necessarily reveal all that is significant in social reality. While draconian potentials exist, their expression is some- what tempered by the public and familiar qualities of the lives of fishers, fish plant workers and fish plant owners/managers in small communities. With few exceptions, all are well known to one another. Born and raised in the same place, owners/managers, attended the local schools and churches, played at the same ac- tivities, experienced the same community events as other residents. Consequently, as one plant owner noted:

> I live here too, you know. I was raised here. I've known these people
> all my life. We do our best for them. Got to. Otherwise how would
> you walk down the street and look anyone in the eye.

Paternalistic patronage in small social communities of familiars is associated with responsibilities for the patrons and expectations on behalf of the clients. On the basis of relations of familiarity, patrons are expected to treat and deal with clients fairly and reasonably. As a consequence, draconian expressions of discretion- ary power are contained and tempered, but certainly neither eliminated nor, in some instances, unexercised.

FISH MARKETING

Digby Neck and the Islands fish processors produce a variety of products that are directed to a number of markets. Three of these processors have specialised in fresh fish production. All of their product is moved, under contract, to major corporate players in the

Nova Scotian fishing industry, either the Digby Town plant of National Sea Products Ltd. or Comeau Seafoods Ltd.[5] The remaining processors sell their products in American and Canadian markets. The northeastern United States, especially the Boston area, receives most of the fresh fish and lobster. Some fresh fish and most of the salt fish is sold to Nova Scotia-based wholesale firms. Several processors have made preliminary efforts to develop markets elsewhere in Canada and the world, but these initiatives have yet to come to fruition. Consequently the independent processors are overwhelmingly dependent upon the United States market. While fishers are generally price-takers vis-à-vis the local processors, the processors in turn are price-takers in their markets. In these markets they compete not only with American supply but also with European and other non-North American products.

To complicate matters further, the political dimension adds uncertainty to the position of Canadian suppliers to the American market. The dependence upon this market has grown steadily since the end of World War II. Two developments led to the present situation. First, the Boston fishermen's strike of 1946 reoriented dealers towards obtaining an even larger supply from Canadian sources. Second, a series of decisions since the end of World War II denied the American industry tariffs or other relief from imports. These developments resulted in the Atlantic Canadian fishery becoming even more intertwined with the northeastern United States market.

In the new situation of a 200 mile exclusive economic zone, both Canadian and US fishers foresaw relief from the foreign fleets which had dominated the fisheries in the 1960s and 1970s. Both fleets expanded and modernised in anticipation of a bonanza which has failed to materialise. Beginning with jurisdictional dispute over access to Georges Bank, there has been increasing pressure from interest groups in the United States to restrict Canadian imports of fish. Claims of unfair competition through subsidies have been exacerbated by the drop in the value of the Canadian dollar against the US dollar which has increased the competitiveness of Canadian fisheries' production in the US market. One of the mechanisms set up by the American government to help its fisheries—regional fisheries councils—has provided a more unified and effective lobby than hitherto available for American fisheries interests. Thus, the Atlantic fisheries, and with it the Digby Neck and the Islands industry, finds itself more vulnerable to possible changes in US policy than ever before.

The Development of the Small Boat Dragger Fleet   4

In major fishing harbours on Digby Neck and the Islands, Cape Island Boats and the distinctive high-bowed Cape St. Mary's ground-fish draggers are often found together, moored on "joans" (harbour anchor buoys) or tied to wharves. The Cape Islander appears more rudimentary, more spartan and less technically endowed than the Cape St. Mary's Boat. From the curving sweep of its pilot house windows to the winches, iron superstructure and perched trawl doors on its deck, the Cape St. Mary's small dragger seems an ocean thoroughbred compared with the work horse disposition of the Cape Island Boat. Indeed, this contrast mirrors the major organisational and developmental features of the Digby Neck and the Islands fisheries. Compared with the multi-purpose Cape Islander, the small boat dragger is the new kid on the block—entering the picture late in the 1940s. In fact, the first draggers were nothing more than converted Cape Island Boats. From such modest beginnings small dragger technologies developed to the point that by the late 1960s they had attained their current position as the most cost efficient and productive fishing boat in Atlantic Canada (see Charron 1977). Through the process of its development, the small boat dragger has fundamentally contributed to the transformation of the Digby Neck and the Islands fisheries and, as a consequence, to the socio-economic dilemma currently confronting the industry.[1]

Isolating causality is frequently a major objective in the social study of technological innovation and development. It is generally anticipated that identifiable conditions exist to explain why certain events and developments occur. In the case of the small boat dragger, isolating causality involves appreciating the complexities and interplay of socio-economic conditions and opportunity. Of course, these factors by themselves, while necessary, are basically insufficient. In addition, there must be individuals well-situated in the socio-economic environment, who are able to recognize opportunity and are motivated to risk learning a new, essentially foreign, technology. This necessary combination of individuals, conditions and opportunity dovetailed in East Ferry, Digby Neck during the late 1940s.

THE INTRODUCTION OF THE SMALL BOAT DRAGGER

Until the late 1940s the Digby Neck and Islands small boat fishery appeared no different from that of other parts of southwest Nova Scotia, with the exception of the specific adjustments in fishing strategies, work organisation and technological approaches requisite to exploiting fish stocks in the St. Mary's Bay and the Bay of Fundy marine environments. Fishers used hook and line, lobster trap, and net technologies out of owner/operator Cape Island Boats. They sold their catches to one buyer who provided credit to outfit them for various fisheries. In return, fishers were obligated to sell their catches to the debt-holding buyers. Fishers caught in this relationship were price-takers while fish buyers were price-givers. Moreover, the prices received for fish during the mid '40s were dismal. Several fishers reported prices such as $1.50 for every hundred pounds of cod, $2.00 per hundred of haddock, $.50 per hundred of pollock, $.30 per hundred of hake and $.25–30 per pound for lobster. Buyers throughout Digby Neck and the Islands gave similar prices. Even fishers with economic independence would be hard pressed to realise any income advantage from their ability to sell to the highest bidder. At these prices only consistent production of tremendous catches would leave fishers with meaningful income surpluses over the costs of operating a fishing enterprise and supporting a household.

While such socio-economic conditions are not generally conducive to risk-taking and technological experimentation, the hope of a decent income from increased productivity could motivate fishers to take chances. Several men from one East Ferry family were motivated to try a foreign technology introduced by a Norwegian fisher.

The German invasion of Norway stranded numerous Norwegian fishers and sailors, a number of whom crossed the Atlantic and settled in Maritime Canadian ports. One of these, Svein Gillson, a man who had fished on draggers for many years, married Elizabeth Rouseau, the daughter of an East Ferry fishing family and settled there. At first, Gillson tried to establish a herring processing facility at Mink Cove. When this failed, he and a partner, an East Ferry fisher/fish buyer, obtained a small boat and rigged it to go fish dragging. Although tentative and not altogether successful, this first

effort demonstrated the potential of fish dragging to local fishers—
especially to the Gillson's wife's cousins, Stan and Rod Rouseau. As
Stan observed, "My brother and I got started about a month or so
after that. Rigged a boat up and tried it out."

Unlike many fishers, the Rouseaus were relatively unencum-
bered by debt obligations to any one fish buyer and were able to seize
this new opportunity. They started fishing at an early age and by
their fourteenth birthdays they were fishing full-time as crew in their
father's gasoline boat. They went longline and lobster fishing with
him. As Stan described it:

> He was basic to our start. He taught us all about the ground for
> lobsterin' and longline fishin'. He showed us how to rig gear, how
> to use gear and how to repair and care for a boat.

In the substance of his relationship with his sons as crewmen-
apprentices, their father was basically similar to other fathers, but
differed from others in the management of his business affairs. Stan
Rouseau observed that, while his father had an account with a fish
buyer, "He never was one to borrow much. Believed that it's best to
pay as you go." The Rouseaus' father "always sold around," seeking
the best available prices for his catches. He transmitted to his sons
beliefs in the values of hard work, independence, a job well done,
and an acumen in the management of business affairs. Stan and
Rod Rouseau quickly put these beliefs into practice after purchasing
their own boats and gear.

Stan reported that he had difficulty keeping crewmen:

> They never agreed with what I did. They never wanted to go as hard
> as I wanted to go. Seemed like I had a different man every year.

The work described by Stan leaves little wonder that some men
might have had difficulties with his approach:

> We'd start in the spring fishin' in St. Mary's Bay. Usually from about
> mid-March to the last week of April. Then we'd begin fishin' trawl
> in the Bay of Fundy. We'd fish two tides everyday. We'd go from
> before day light to after dark for at least six weeks. Usually by
> mid-June we'd be offshore in the Bay of Fundy after hake. We used
> to stick at this until sometime around the end of October. Then
> we'd go back to haddockin' until the lobster season. If there wasn't
> anything goin' in lobsterin' we'd get right back to haddock fishing.
> It was drive, drive, drive!

Stan financed his first boat through a no-interest loan from an
East Ferry fish buyer. The buyer extended the loan as leverage to
assure access to Stan's fish, known to be copious in quantity and
good in quality. But, by the time he had sold it two years later the

loan was paid and he had generated enough savings to substantially reduce the fish buyer's contribution to the next boat—a three-year-old, 38'11" Cape Islander, powered by a new straight eight cylinder Buick gasoline engine. He rigged this boat for the first attempts at fish dragging. An attitude stressing hard work and independence, combined with a business acumen and the fortuitous marriage of their cousin to a knowledgeable Norwegian dragger fisher, provided Stan and his brother with the means and motivation to take up the challenge and the promise of a foreign fishing technology.

The Rouseau brothers enlisted the aid of the Norwegian. He helped them rig the boat and gear, and taught them the correct way to assemble the numerous components of trawl gear. At first Gillson even went out with them. He taught the Rouseaus how to handle and fish a drag net: that is, how to select appropriate ocean bottom, how to keep the trawl doors properly placed, the speed of tows and hauling back. Stan described the arrangement in the following manner:

> I paid for everything. All he [Gillson] had to do was show me how to rig it and how to fish it. For doin' this he got half of whatever we caught and sold. This lasted as long as I needed him in order to learn the business.

The Rouseaus learned quickly. Without either radar or bottom echo sounders, they used devices such as flares to light up their tows. They also shared experiences and acquired knowledge about the peculiarities of fishing drag nets on particular pieces of ocean bottom. Soon the catches were filling their holds.

These men approached working a drag net with the same vigour they had employed with other gears. "We'd drag all night and sell over in Belliveau Cove. Then we'd drag all day and sell in East Ferry." Again they had difficulty in keeping crew men. Most did not agree with the demands placed on their time and labour, regardless of how hard the captains themselves worked. Nonetheless the Rouseau brothers persisted, quickly establishing small boat fish dragging as a permanent feature of the Digby Neck and the Islands fishery. They even helped other men rig their boats and gear, providing general advice while retaining much of the particular, experientially-based, knowledge necessary to assembling and successfully using drag nets in the marine environment.

At first fish dragging was a summer season activity restricted to St. Mary's Bay. The boats, rigged-over Cape Islanders, were small and underpowered. Only St. Mary's Bay provided protection from heavy seas, as well as expansive areas of relatively flat bottom, the only conditions that would permit such boats to work drag nets. As a Tiverton fisher noted,

> Then there was plenty of fish in St. Mary's Bay— flounder, haddock, cod, catfish. You could make a go of it there then.

During the rest of the year they still went longlining and lobster fishing.

In 1952 Stan Rouseau bought a new boat for $8,000—a 42 foot long, 14 foot wide Cape Island type hull outfitted with a six cylinder GMC diesel on a reduction gear. She was also equipped with radar and sounding machinery; a state of the art vessel for the time. This boat had the size, power and equipment to fish grounds outside of St. Mary's Bay. Instead of obtaining assistance from a fish buyer, Stan paid one-third down and financed the rest with a subsidized loan from the government. This was his first experience with governmental assistance; notably, provided only after he had arranged to have letters of reference sent by fish dealers and bank managers outlining his qualifications and financial condition. This boat was designed to allow continued participation in the longline and lobster fisheries. As Stan remarked, "We still weren't certain drag fishing was goin' to last. So, we wanted to be able to do other things in case it failed." Failure was not in the cards.

After 1954, weather permitting, Stan Rouseau was fish dragging year-round. He fished from St. Mary's Bay down to Trinity Ledge from March until about mid-June, then shifted to the Bay of Fundy until the following March. He fished the Bay of Fundy shore from Digby to below Brier Island. Fish dragging had emerged as a specialised and entrenched form of small boat groundfishing by the mid '50s. This did not occur without considerable opposition from hook and line fishers. As one dragger captain noted:

> A lot of fishermen were opposed to drag fishing. They claimed it killed small fish and broke the stocks down. I knew they was right. I was a ground fisherman myself. I had done a lot of hook and line fishin'. I went drag fishin' anyway. I don't think that with proper management we'd be any better off than we are today.

Several hook and line fishers claimed that the destruction of enormous quantities of small fish was such an integral aspect of fish dragging that the early boats fishing in St. Mary's Bay had a special holding bin into which catches were dumped. "The good ones were picked out and all the trash let go over the stern through a special chute built into the bin for that purpose." Today, older men point to the dearth of groundfish in St. Mary's Bay and the Bay of Fundy as proof of the correctness of their position. As one retired Tiverton fisher proclaimed:

> Once you could make a livin', a good livin' fishin' linetrawl in St. Mary's Bay. Many men did. Right off of here. Now you couldn't catch one. They're gone, destroyed by fish draggin'. Not just the fish mind you, the bottom too. All sand now. The same has been happenin' to the Bay of Fundy. Every year for a long while now there has been less and less fish for the inshore line fishermen. Why one time hake fishin' was a big thing here. Twenty, thirty boats from here alone all goin' out into the Bay of Fundy for hake. Now there's two here that could go and one of those just lays tied to the Joan. I tell ya its completely gone and we've got the draggers to thank for it.

FLEET GROWTH AND DEVELOPMENT

At first the build-up of the small boat dragger fleet was gradual. Its development was essentially unregulated until the first federal licences and regulations designed specifically for this fishing effort began to appear in the late '50s and early '60s. Early in 1956 a fisheries officer reported that only eight draggers were fishing out of the Digby Neck and Islands area.[2] Seven of these were 40 foot boats mainly operating in St. Mary's Bay, but the eighth was one of the new, technically equipped and powerfully driven 60 foot vessels. The appearance of this class of vessel signalled the development of a specialised and mobile fishing machine able to exploit distant as well as nearshore grounds year-round. By late 1962 there were 25 draggers in the fleet. Many of those were still in the 40 foot class, but the shift to the larger, more technically proficient fish dragger was well underway. In January 1963 a fisheries officer reported that:

> The only difference [in the small boat dragger fleet] being three 40 ft. class draggers were replaced by 65 ft. vessels and one 54 ft. converted. There is a strong tendency toward 55 ft. and 65 ft. class draggers at this time but fishermen report that it is very difficult to get builders to accept their orders (*Annual Narrative Reports* 1963).

While the size of the dragger fleet was peaking, its technical character was undergoing rapid change. By now the small boat dragger was a specialised technology with a distinctive hull and superstructure design—the Cape St. Mary's type of vessel.[3] It contained the latest models in electronic aids, such as an echo sounder (fish finder), radar and Loran A (a navigation/location identification device). A new, completely outfitted, wooden hull fish dragger cost between $50,000 and $60,000 during the early '60s, a princely sum for fishers obtaining $.06 a pound for haddock, $.04 a pound for cod and $.02 a pound for pollock. Regardless, the reluctance of boat builders to accept new orders for larger draggers clearly reflects the demand for this type of boat. Apparently the production potential of such vessels more than compensated for the dismal fish prices. What fishers could not earn from quality prices, they could make up through high volume landings.

These developmental trends continued until the early '70s, when the general collapse of fish stocks, in particular haddock, from over-exploitation in Atlantic Canada resulted in a dramatic reduction in the number of small boat draggers fishing out of Digby Neck and the Islands ports. By 1972 only 16 vessels of this type were operating. However, the condition was short-lived. The fleet began to build again following the recovery of fish stocks and the 1977 Canadian declaration of the 200 mile exclusive economic zone. In 1983 there were 35 small boat draggers fishing out of Digby Neck and the Islands, most of them over 50 feet in length.

While the hull design has remained more or less the same since the '60s, many aspects of fish dragging technology have changed or become even more technically sophisticated. The pilot house of the '80s small dragger resembles a cockpit with a vast array of primary and back-up electronic instrumentation. In addition to engine function gauges, most boats contain at least two radar units, a wet and dry paper echo sounder, two Loran C units, an automatic pilot, a couple of UHF radios and CBs, and a plotter (an electronic device interfaced with a Loran C unit which actually plots the course of each net tow). Most of these boats have also adopted a particular otter trawl design referred to as "western trawl." Fully rigged and equipped for fishing, a new 60 foot wooden-hull vessel costs in excess of $500,000. Steel-hulled models sell for over $1 million. Fishing with this technology, which once required a princely sum, now demands a king's ransom. The explosive growth in the dragger fleet since the late '50s and, in particular, its dramatic technical development, was closely associated with two factors: the imperatives of fish buyers/processors and the accessibility of government financing and subsidisation to fishers. Fish buyers were successfully cultivating northeastern United States markets for fresh fish as well as changing their processing orientation from salt fish to fresh fish fillets. Consequently, they had a vested interest in encouraging and, in many instances, participating in the development of fish catching techniques that would provide them with high volume supplies of groundfish, especially haddock (the fish of preference for the fresh markets). In fact, the Digby Neck and the Islands fish processing industry was undergoing structural and technical changes in concert with the fish catching sector (see Chapter 6). Closely linked to these changes were the appearance and development of federal and provincial programmes which provided fishers with a combination of subsidy and low interest loan arrangements whereby they could finance the purchase of new boats and equipment. The crucial linkages between the imperatives of fish processors, fishers' access to financing through government programmes, and the growth of the dragger fleet will be outlined and discussed in greater detail later in this study.

The Impact of Small Boat Draggers on the Digby Neck and the Islands Fishery

5

The conflict between hook and line fishers and drag net fishers, which was alluded to earlier, is on the surface, an expected outcome of competition between different technical approaches to the exploitation of a common property resource. While true that the earlier small, underpowered, drag net operation was restricted to fishing ocean bottom which was relatively smooth and sheltered (e.g., St. Mary's Bay), technological advances soon made it possible for dragger operations to exploit many grounds fished by longline and handline fishers. The resulting conflict among fishers, many of whom come from the same community and social backgrounds, originates in the fundamental incompatibility of the technologies. Longline is a set gear, drag nets are mobile gear. At best, they can exploit the same ground at the same time without consequence only if dragger captains are very attentive to the course of their tows, and are willing to divert fishing activity away from set gear. The onus is on the dragger captains because their technology is mobile.

Digby Neck and the Islands hook and line fishers have complained about drag net fishing from its outset. Often these complaints were made directly to federal fisheries officers. For instance, in 1955 one fisheries officer reported receiving numerous complaints from line fishers that their lines were being interfered with by draggers (*Narrative Reports* 1955).[1] There are similar reports in many of the succeeding years.[2]

The opposition of line fishers to drag net fishing has a long and tumultuous history in Maritime Canada. During the 1920s an industry-wide protest against the introduction and deployment of beam trawlers was so successful that a federally appointed Royal Commission investigating the matter brought forth recommendations which would in effect freeze the size of the trawling fleet (Royal

Commission Investigating the Fisheries 1928). These recommendations were adopted by the federal government. Drag net fishing remained strictly regulated until the early 1940s. World War II and the war effort drive to industrialise the entire economy, including food production, resulted in the easing of regulations. Thereafter the large trawler fleet rapidly expanded. With these changes came the modernisation/industrialisation policy thrusts of various levels of government concerning fisheries development.[3]

Until the early '60s the Digby Neck and the Islands small boat dragger fleet developed essentially outside of government regulatory view, but the opposition to it and the complaints about it, especially on the part of line fishers, had many features in common with the earlier resistance to beam trawlers. As reported in the fisheries officer's *Annual Narrative Reports*, these line fishers complained that dragging killed small fish, destroyed ocean bottom habitats, broke up fish shoals and overexploited stocks. It was argued that such consequences, coupled with the mobile character of drag net operations, forced line fishers to fish only those marine environments inaccessible to draggers. Many also argued that draggers landed such large catches in the port market that they exerted downward pressure on fish prices. In short, line fishers strongly felt that dragger fishing eroded the basis of their livelihoods (*Narrative Reports*, various years). Today, many Digby Neck and the Islands line fishers articulate the same arguments in their explanation of the conditions underlying the dilemma facing their fishery and livelihoods. For instance, one fisher claims,

> They've [small boat draggers] ruined it for everyone, including themselves. Too many small fish have been destroyed, too much bottom tore up.

Another fisher argues,

> The draggers have fished themselves out of business, and with themselves lots of others. Ya can't just dip, dip, dip and hope there'll always be fish to replace the ones ya take. After awhile its got to catch up with ya.

A Westport fisher noted that,

> The draggers clean the bottom, often before we get much of a chance. All that's left to us is the really hard bottom [extremely rocky with large outcrops and boulders], places they can't go. Now, with the new rock hopper trawl, we're even seeing draggers there. Soon we'll be pushed right out of it. Draggers have ruined it. Soon they'll have nothin' to catch and they'll be tied up at the dock like the rest of us.

DEMISE OF THE LINE FISHERY

Without question the advent and development of small boat fish draggers has had a resounding impact on the Digby Neck and the Islands fishery. Table 5 outlines the weights and values of the major groundfish species landed in Digby Neck and the Islands ports between 1952 and 1983. As these data demonstrate, landed weights for species such as cod and haddock leapt substantially by the mid '60s. For instance, in 1965 cod landings were over 120 percent higher than those recorded for 1952 and haddock landings were fully 261 percent higher than those reported for 1952. Conversely, by 1965 hake landings had declined from the 1952 figure by almost 82 percent. The growth in cod and haddock landings corresponds directly with the increased use of the small boat draggers while the collapse in hake landings indicate either a shift away from hake as the species of preference in the hook and line fishery, or a collapse in the stocks.[4]

In December 1966, the senior fisheries officer in District 37 reported that:

> Hake, one of the chief species that supported this line fishery through the years, have practically disappeared. Since 1963 the overall landings of Hake have dropped approximately 80 percent (*Narrative Reports* 1966).

Here the officer is arguing that the stocks collapsed. Some line fishers agree with him, asserting that the damage drag fishing wrought to ocean habitats destroyed the basis of the hake fishery. Earlier in 1966, the same fisheries officer described developments in the fishery which at least partially supported the line fishers' contention:

> There is still a large percentage of the local fishermen operating with hook and line but they are gradually being replaced by draggers. At the present time draggers are few in numbers but they account for approximately 75 percent of the total landings. The old hook and line method of fishing could possibly be classed as a soft spot in the commercial fishery. This method appears to produce fewer fish each year. Because modern methods and fishermen are taking over the grounds where the line fishermen have operated for years [sic]. This has forced them to fish nearer the shore or in areas where draggers cannot operate (*Narrative Reports* 1966).

Increasing drag net fishing forced hook and line fishers to exploit less productive grounds that were inaccessible to draggers. This fisheries officer was of the opinion that hook and line groundfishing had been dramatically reduced by the dragger fleet. According to his report, by 1966 dragger fishers had replaced hook and line fishers

TABLE 5: Landed Weights (000's lbs.) and Landed Values ($000's) for Selected Groundfish Species, Digby Neck and the Islands (District 37), 1952–1983.

	Groundfish Species							
	Cod		Haddock		Pollock		Hake	
Year	Landed Weight	Landed Value	Landed Weight	Landed Value	Landed Weight	Landed Value	Landed Weight	Landed Value
1952	2831	91	2179	119	3543	79	5805	135
1953	2467	65	3275	140	4258	75	5874	105
1954	2678	78	2367	121	4712	77	6518	121
1955	3152	95	3494	149	4673	93	5790	116
1956	3756	113	4501	212	4351	87	5555	127
1957	3017	94	4159	198	7184	169	6054	162
1958	2414	88	3815	232	6127	128	3686	95
1959	2901	108	3506	217	4141	108	4730	133
1960	2953	102	3291	173	9414	250	3264	93
1961	2950	115	3774	231	4823	126	3561	113
1962	3792	153	6980	385	8844	310	2889	97
1963	3330	151	8677	492	9729	357	3519	134
1964	4950	235	7590	476	5363	213	2786	113
1965	6249	315	7858	586	4312	180	1049	43
1966	6779	384	16146	1206	4760	204	651	30
1967	8002	415	12005	704	3241	131	579	28
1968	6826	357	9905	750	5599	200	894	45
1969	5383	325	6185	639	5017	195	980	33
1970	4033	331	4395	601	3337	157	859	36
1971	3202	298	3088	421	2972	172	1074	55
1972	3903	383	2502	463	4024	240	1985	119
1973	2819	322	1760	360	10629	651	2517	161
1974	3155	398	3217	650	6835	483	2677	202
1975	3821	397	5068	869	6717	390	2597	157
1976	3111	381	3627	1734	7385	466	1839	128
1977	7033	932	4621	1021	6409	513	1351	105
1978	5496	835	8501	1806	4341	411	1462	154
1979	5769	1124	7948	1858	8067	1156	1759	277
1980	6404	1378	8724	2381	8353	1288	1945	286
1981	7540	1657	8536	1851	6517	1060	1488	248
1982	9365	2316	8093	2189	7685	1397	1964	336
1983	11023	2419	9632	3121	8406	1116	1561	157

Source: Department of Fisheries and Oceans, Statistical Branch.

as the primary producers of groundfish in the Digby Neck and the Islands fishing industry.

Ironically, in the late 1960s and early 1970s, the collapse of groundfish stocks reduced the numbers of fish draggers and the dragger effort, opening up opportunities for line fishers. In a situation of reduced fish stocks, line fishing becomes more effective and cost efficient. But the respite was short-lived. With the gradual improvement in fish stocks through the early and mid '70s the dragger fleet started to rebuild, this time with a vengeance. The consequences for fish landings are evident in Table 5. By 1985, cod landings in District 37 totalled over 11 million pounds, almost a threefold increase over the 1973 low of 2,819,000 pounds. Haddock landings show an even greater increase over this period—by 1983 they were almost four times higher than those reported for 1972.[5] These data suggest that fish landings in Digby Neck and the Islands are fast approaching the level of productivity associated with the late '60s collapse of fish stocks.[6]

Table 6 profiles the percentage of total landings of the major groundfish species accounted for by coastal zone, inshore effort, primarily hook and line fishers.[7] With the exception of increased shares in total landings reported for 1980 and 1981, the inshore sector has experienced a gradual and persistent erosion since the mid '70s in its portion of total landings. In fact, the data for the last two years indicate that the inshore groundfishing sector is in the process of completely collapsing. At the end of 1983, the inshore sector accounted for only 9.0 percent of cod landings, 4.9 percent of haddock landings, 4.7 percent of pollock landings and, remarkably, only 37.9 percent of hake landings. This latter statistic is particularly telling since hake fishing was once the major line fishery. Moreover, the data for the other species clearly indicate that line fishers are not simply shifting their effort from hake fishing to other groundfish. During the summer of 1984, many line fishers confirmed the prevalence of this condition in the coastal zone groundfishery. Most attribute it to the growth and fishing effort of small boat draggers. One line fisher argued:

> First they stripped St. Mary's Bay. Then, when the bigger boats started comin' in, they moved out into the Bay of Fundy and other grounds. Now they're startin' in on the deep water in the Bay of Fundy, one of the only places left where we can fish. No, there's not much left for us. They catch'em all up before we get a chance. With this new rock-hopper trawl soon they'll be fishin' up and around the Ridge and the few remainin' places we can go.

TABLE 6: Coastal Zone Landings as a % of Total Landed Weights for Selected Groundfish Species, Digby Neck and the Islands (District 37), 1967–1983

	Groundfish Species			
	Cod	Haddock	Pollock	Hake
Year	%	%	%	%
1967	31.0	8.2	22.9	96.9
1968	26.4	10.0	23.4	80.0
1964	31.3	23.4	24.6	70.9
1970	36.9	21.1	18.1	84.5
1971	6.3	11.8	18.8	83.0
1972	29.8	17.0	5.8	93.7
1973	37.3	17.8	7.5	94.8
1974	36.4	10.6	16.2	94.7
1975	38.8	8.5	12.0	97.5
1976	37.3	6.1	12.1	98.0
1977	21.9	7.9	13.9	96.6
1978	19.6	3.0	9.4	96.7
1979	27.8	3.6	15.5	84.7
1980	38.8	12.0	17.7	88.0
1981	34.4	12.5	7.8	94.0
1982	18.9	6.6	9.0	62.7
1983	9.0	4.9	4.7	37.9

Source: Department of Fisheries and Oceans, Statistical Branch.

While the small boat dragger fleet based at Digby Neck and the Islands may not be the only cause of the collapse of the hook and line fishery, many line fishers emphatically believe it to be responsible. Compounding this situation is the dearth of viable alternatives to the groundfishery. For instance, herring fishing with weirs and gill nets at one time provided an alternative or, at least, a supplement to groundfishing. Yet as Table 7 indicates, while the coastal zone sector currently accounts for the majority of herring landings, the collapse of stocks as well as the fall in prices has denied the majority of inshore fishers the ability to turn to the herring fishery for a substantial portion of their livelihoods. Lobster fishing represents the sole activity through which coastal zone fishers can attempt to compensate for the income losses from line fishing.

Table 8 outlines the landed weights, landed values, and average price per pound between 1952 and 1983 for the Digby Neck and the Islands lobster fishery. These data indicate increased landings during the 1982 and 1983 seasons. This might indicate increased effort, but it may also simply reflect a point on the upward side of the cyclical swings in lobster populations, as is evident in the data

TABLE 7: Coastal Zone Herring Landings as a % of Total Herring Landings, (000's lbs.) Digby Neck and the Islands (District 37), 1967–1983

Year	Inshore Percentage of Total Landings (%)	Total Landings (000's lbs.)
1967	19.5	46,340
1968	10.1	40,790
1969	11.9	30,698
1970	31.8	16,426
1971	38.9	15,697
1972	24.5	12,841
1973	28.3	29,733
1974	16.3	23,310
1975	12.9	26,230
1976	56.8	6,625
1977	100.0	2,266
1978	88.3	5,844
1979	55.0	3,598
1980	62.3	2,714
1981	91.8	4,687
1982	85.1	2,610
1983	87.2	2,264

Source: Department of Fisheries and Oceans, Statistical Branch.

for earlier years. However, given the groundfishery and herring situation, there is no question that coastal zone fishers are now forced to place a much greater emphasis upon lobster fishing. In fact, many of these fishers are approaching virtual dependence upon this fishery for their earned livelihoods. This means that a form of fish production which once drew its vitality from an ability and need to pursue various fisheries is now quickly moving toward a specialised focus on the lobster fishery. Considering that lobster fishing is a federally regulated activity restricted to a specific time of the year, the Digby Neck and the Islands coastal zone fishery has been largely transformed into a seasonal, part-time pursuit.[8] As one older Freeport coastal zone fisher noted:

> Many of the boats here make up what we call the mosquito fleet. Part-timers that run around here and there handlinin' the odd fish, some of 'em just puttin' in time until lobsterin' begins.

Many small boat dragger fishers are aware of and sensitive to the situation facing coastal zone fishers. After all, not so long ago either they or their fathers were part of that fishery. Often they are the first to acknowledge the role of the small boat dragger in the

TABLE 8: Landed Weights (000's lbs.) and Landed Values ($000's) for Lobster, Digby Neck and the Islands (District 37), 1952–1983

Year	Landed Weight 000's lbs.	Landed Value $000's	Average Price Per lb. $
1952	579	265	.46
1953	649	284	.44
1954	561	261	.47
1955	509	272	.53
1956	627	361	.58
1957	582	278	.48
1958	513	276	.54
1959	602	321	.53
1960	559	256	.46
1961	613	326	.53
1962	642	384	.60
1963	751	491	.65
1964	710	538	.76
1965	726	662	.91
1966	689	517	.75
1967	696	555	.80
1968	774	584	.75
1969	1142	955	.84
1970	818	820	1.00
1971	844	967	1.15
1972	550	809	1.47
1973	676	1050	1.55
1974	568	847	1.49
1975	620	1120	1.81
1976	463	1003	2.17
1977	653	1514	2.32
1978	487	1500	3.08
1979	602	1586	2.64
1980	461	1497	3.25
1981	549	1705	3.11
1982	609	1949	3.20
1983	800	2794	3.49

Source: Department of Fisheries and Oceans.

past, pre-dragger era, with a sense of nostalgia. They also throw their arms in the air claiming that what is currently happening to coastal zone fishers would be happening to them if they had not gotten involved in drag fishing. A number of them insist that they did not have many options. For instance, one captain, when asked why he entered the dragger fishery, stated:

> It didn't seem I had much of a choice. There wasn't much goin' in the line and herrin' fisheries while things were lookin' pretty good at draggin'. So, it was either do this or get out of it altogether.

Ironically, the apparent impending collapse in fish stocks, particularly haddock, has not passed unnoticed by small dragger captains. Several of them are convinced that their fishery will be the next to fail. Consequently, a number of fishers are currently trying to sell their boats with the stated purpose of buying a Cape Island Boat so that they can go line and/or net fishing. Many of the dragger captains and crewmen already own licensed lobster boats which they use every fall—tying up their draggers to pursue the potentially quick and bountiful dollars of the fall lobster fishery.

IMPACT ON COMMUNITIES

Regardless of the future fate of the small boat dragger, there can be no question that its development has contributed substantially to the permanent transformation of the Digby Neck and the Islands fisheries. Many of these changes have been experienced differentially in the ports along the Neck and on the Islands. Table 9 outlines the fleet structure of the major fishing ports for various years between 1957 and 1983. As can be seen in these data, fish dragging has been concentrated in East Ferry, Little River and Tiverton. In recent years, draggers have also been working out of Freeport and, particularly, Westport. The recent growth of the dragger fleet in Westport may be a sign of things to come. This port contains an ambitious young fish processor who is currently in an expansion phase of development. Dragger fleet increases here are linked to this expansion—a development that is projected by the processor to continue into at least the near future. Centreville, once a significant early locus of fish dragging, has experienced a rapid decline in its fleet from eight vessels in 1967 to one boat by the early '80s. Overall, the dragger portion of the fleet grew by two and a half times between 1957 and 1983.

Since the mid '70s Little River has emerged as the dominant fish dragging port in the area. Between 1957 and 1983 its fleet grew from 3 to 17 vessels—an increase over 450 percent. While other ports

TABLE 9: Fleet Structure by Selected Communities, Digby Neck and the Islands (District 37), for Various Years Between 1957-1983[1]

Communities	1957	1967	1971	1972	1977	1979	1980	1981	1982	1983	% Change 1957–1983
CENTREVILLE											
Draggers	1	8	4	3	N/A	3	1	1	1	1	0
Boats	18	13	16	14	N/A	9	8	8	8	9	-50.0
Other	-	-	-	-	N/A	-	-	-	-	-	-
EAST FERRY											
Draggers	4	5	4	2	N/A	4	6	7	7	5	+25.0
Boats	8	12	11	11	N/A	10	15	10	10	10	+25.0
Other	-	-	-	-	N/A	1	1	-	-	-	-
FREEPORT											
Draggers	-	-	-	1	-	-	-	2	2	2	+200.00
Boats	31	34	37	40	37	25	26	24	25	21	-32.3
Other	4	3	-	1	1	-	-	2	2	2	-50.0
LITTLE RIVER											
Draggers	3	5	7	5	N/A	12	14	14	17	17	+467.0
Boats	15	17	20	27	N/A	15	14	13	11	11	-26.7
Other	1	-	-	-	N/A	-	-	-	-	0	-
SANDY COVE											
Draggers	-	1	-	-	N/A	-	-	1	-	-	-
Boats	18	19	16	16	N/A	17	14	15	15	14	-22.2
Other	-	-	-	-	N/A	-	-	-	-	-	-
TIVERTON											
Draggers	2	3	3	4	3	4	5	3	4	5	+150.0
Boats	36	23	24	26	24	16	8	19	7	16	-55.6
Other	-	-	-	-	N/A	-	-	-	-	-	-
WESTPORT											
Draggers	-	-	1	1	1	1	2	1	3	5	+500.0
Boats	41	34	32	28	20	25	27	23	28	19	-53.7
Other	2	6	-	1	1	1	4	3	2	-	-100.0
TOTALS											
Draggers	10	22	19	16	N/A	24	30	29	34	35	+250.0
Boats	167	152	156	162	N/A	117	112	112	104	100	-40.1
Other	7	9	0	2	N/A	2	5	5	4	2	-350.0

Source: Department of Fisheries and Oceans.

1. The years represented are the only years for which these data were available.

contain small fish draggers, this port stands alone in terms of the sheer scale of its fleet. The growth and concentration of the dragger fleet in Little River is attributable to two inter-related factors. On the one hand, Little River offered a well-protected harbour augmented by a large government wharf. On the other hand, a number of fish buyers/processors, who had committed themselves at an early stage to fresh fillet production, were located at Little River. Notably, a recently completed federal government harbour development project at Sandy Cove, including comprehensive dredging and an entirely new and extensive wharf, is resulting in a shift of draggers to this port from Little River and East Ferry. In short, the data concerning the development of the dragger fleet reveal growth in specific ports.

The same cannot be said for the small boat fleet. In every port but one, the small boat fleet experienced dramatic declines between 1957 and 1983. In general, there were over 40 percent fewer small boats fishing out of the major ports in 1983 than there were in 1957. Even more dramatic declines in the boat fleet are apparent in Little River and Freeport when one compares the 1983 fleet with that of the early '70s (a 59.3 percent decline in the former and a 47.5 percent decline in the latter). Between 1957 and 1983, the boat fleet in specific communities had declined as follows: Centreville 50 percent, Freeport 32.3 percent, Little River 26.7 percent, Sandy Cove 22.2 percent, Tiverton 55.6 percent and Westport by 53.7 percent. These data clearly mark the decline of the coastal zone fishery—a decline that mirrors the growth of the dragger fleet and the demise of the line fishery. In places such as Centreville, Freeport, Tiverton and Westport the contemporary boat fleet is a mere shadow of its former self. Indeed, Centreville is on the verge of extinction as a fishing port. Considered with the fact that many of the existing boats are fished either by part-timers or, at least, seasonally in the lobster fishery, it certainly appears that the coastal zone fishery as it was earlier constituted is nearing its end.

It could be argued that the change in fleet structure signifies no more than line fishers' switching to another technology. While it is true that during the early years dragger fishers did come from a line and coastal zone fishing background, the decline of the boat fishery was part of a larger, more systematic process than simply fishers changing technologies and approaches. Table 10 outlines the number of fishers by full-time and part-time status for the major fishing ports on Digby Neck and the Islands for selected years between 1957 and 1983. These data reveal the impact of change in the fisheries. By 1983, there were 35.7 percent fewer fishers working out of these ports than reported for 1957. As could be expected from the discus-

Table 10: Number of Fishermen by Status (Full-time=ft., Part-time=pt., Total = t)[1] in Selected Communities, Digby Neck and the Islands (District 37) for Various Years[2]

Communities	Years and Status 1957[3]			1972[4]			1980			1983			% Change 1957-1983 (total)	% Change 1972-1983		
	ft	pt	t	ft	pt	t	ft	pt	t	ft	pt	t		ft	pt	t
Centreville	-	-	67	28	14	42	14	9	23	12	7	19	-71.6	-57.1	-50.0	-54.8
Sandy Cove	-	-	54	29	9	38	14	17	31	24	7	31	-42.6	-17.2	-22.2	-18.4
Little River	-	-	38	27	21	48	31	19	50	54	14	68	+79.0	+100.0	-33.3	+41.7
East Ferry	-	-	27	15	10	25	18	2	20	18	6	24	-11.1	+20.0	-40.0	-4.0
Tiverton	-	-	114	39	13	52	26	22	48	33	19	52	-54.4	-15.4	+46.2	0.0
Freeport	-	-	103	50	20	70	21	31	52	23	18	41	-60.2	-54.0	-10.0	-41.4
Westport	-	-	116	50	8	58	51	24	75	75	24	99	-14.7	-50.0	+200.0	+70.7
Total	-	-	519	238	95	333	175	124	299	239	95	334	-35.7	+0.4	0.0	+0.3

Source: Department of Fisheries and Oceans, Statistics Branch.

1. Status is a category developed by the Department of Fisheries and Oceans (DFO) to measure extent of participation. (See *Annual Statistical Review of Canadian Fisheries*, Department of Fisheries and Oceans, various years for a detailed explanation). While defined in various ways through the years, it most frequently reflects either length of participation through the years or income dependence. For example, those men deriving less than 75% have been classified as part-time. The category was, no doubt, initially developed to assist DFO policy makers access, design and apply licensing programmes when management interventions accelerated during the late '60s.

2. 1957 and 1972 are the only two years available prior to 1980.

3. The data do not distinguish between full-time and part-time for this year.

4. Fishermen categorised as 'occasional' (e.g., less than 50% of income or less than five months of the year) are collapsed into the part-time category. DFO altered its basis for including men in this category through various years. Moreover, status classification often affects access to resources such as new licences, licence renewals, boat and equipment loans/subsidies and so on. That is, priority access is given to those classified as full-time. Consequently, the link between access and status classification frequently compelled men to strive towards or create the illusion of full-time participation. Needless to say management practices on the part of DFO have often been disruptive to local-level community and familial/personal life.

sion of changes in fleet structure, this decline has been experienced differentially in the various ports. Compared with 1957, by 1983 the number of fishers in various ports had declined as follows: Centreville 71.6 percent, Sandy Cove 42.6 percent, Tiverton 54.4 percent and in Freeport 60.2 percent. East Ferry and Westport experienced less dramatic declines of 11.1 percent and 14.7 percent respectively. Only Little River, the centre of small boat dragging, has experienced growth in the number of persons fishing. There were fully 79 percent more persons fishing out of Little River in 1983 then there had been in 1957. Notably, the increases in actual numbers of fishers in Little River do not approach the decreases in fishing populations in the other ports. As evident in Table 10, in 1983 there were only 30 more persons fishing out of Little River than reported in 1957, while by 1983, there were 185 fewer persons participating in the fisheries in the major ports. Obviously, the revolution in the boat fleet described earlier, as well as the decline of the line and inshore groundfisheries, cannot be simply explained as fishers shifting from one fishing technology to another.

Between 1972 and 1983 the total number of fishers in Digby Neck and the Islands remained more or less stable, but several ports continued to experience a decline in numbers while others experienced growth. That is, Centreville, Sandy Cove, Tiverton and Freeport lost fishers during the 1972 to 1983 period; Little River, East Ferry and Westport gained fishers during this decade. Of course these latter ports are the ones within which the development and growth of the small boat dragger has been concentrated. These data reveal a major feature of the impact of the development of the dragger fleet and the decline of the line boat fisheries upon the social and economic profile of the fishery. Centreville, Sandy Cove, Tiverton and Freeport are now on the verge of disappearing as significant line and coastal zone fishing ports. The fisheries, in particular ground-fishing, are concentrated in three ports: East Ferry, Westport and, most significantly, Little River. Moreover, the rise of the small boat dragger fishery has translated into an overall reduction in the number of vessels and the number of fishers—a reduction that has especially affected specific communities. Many of the remaining coastal zone boat operations now participate on either a seasonal or part-time basis. The shift from line fishing to drag net fishing has dramatically increased overall productivity per fisher. On a per fisher basis, almost two and one-half times more pounds of the major groundfish species were landed in 1983 than in 1952.[9] Yet this increased productivity is neither expressed in increased total employment in the fisheries, nor is it evenly distributed among the communities on Digby Neck and the Islands.

But, while the total number of fishers has declined, one might expect that the dramatic increases in total landed weights would contribute to an expansion of employment opportunities in fish processing, thereby absorbing some of the labour displaced from fish catching. However, this has not been the case. Full-time employment in fish processing has declined over the last ten years. For instance, a 1975 study reported that Digby Neck and the Islands fish buyers and processors employed a maximum of 343 full-time workers (MacPherson 1976). Three years later, maximum full-time employment in fish processing was reported to be 298 persons, a decline of 15 percent over the 1975 figures (Province of Nova Scotia 1978). In 1981, 245 persons indicated in the census that they were employed in the manufacturing sector (*Census of Canada* 1981). Since fish processing is the only major manufacturing activity located in the Digby Neck and the Islands area, this number represents the maximum employment sustained by the processing sector in 1981. Overall, these data indicate that between 1975 and 1981 full-time employment in fish processing had declined by as much as 29 percent.

It is apparent that employment lost in fish catching was not made up by an increase in fish processing employment opportunities. Indeed, fish processing was undergoing changes similar to those experienced in the fish catching sector. It too was adopting technologies and labour processes which, while dramatically increasing productivity per worker, reduced the total numbers of employees required. Those communities most affected by these changes in employment opportunities are profoundly threatened in terms of their future participation in the fishing industry. Currently, they do not contain many employment opportunities for their residents. Young people, especially, have no choice but to leave in pursuit of work. These developments raise very important questions concerning the socio-economic future of many communities.

Photo: Small boat draggers and Cape Island boats at Tiverton Wharf.
Credit: Anthony Davis

Fish Draggers and Fish Buyers: 6
Systemic Connections in the
Transformation of the Fishery

Fish buying and processing underwent several fundamental changes in concert with the introduction and development of small boat fish dragging technology. During the '40s and most of the '50s, the processing sector produced mainly salt fish products out of groundfish species such as hake, cod and pollock. Haddock was either turned over fresh, for a commission, to Maritime Fish, later National Sea Products, in Digby Town or was trucked to the Boston fresh fish market. Buyers purchasing lobster sold most of their supply to northeastern United States brokers and lobster pound operators. Herring was sold to fish meal and reduction plants. But the central activity in fish processing was salt fish production.

CHANGES IN THE FISH PROCESSING SECTOR

In 1961 there were 23 fish firms operating on Digby Neck and the Islands. Twenty-two of these were open 10 to 12 months of the year. A senior federal fisheries officer in District 37 noted in 1962 that there was a change underway in the processing sector. Many processors were moving from producing salt fish products to the production of fresh and fresh frozen products. However, by the start of 1962 "seventeen salt fish firms with thirty-four dryers still remain in operation; but, these are not producing the same quantities as a few years back" (*Narrative Reports* 1962). Salt fish production was declining in significance by the early '60s. Late in 1966 the same fisheries officer reported that:

> In this District now there is a trend to larger and more modern vessels and ashore the trend is to more modern processing methods. A large percentage of all fish landings now are processed

fresh and shipped out frozen. A very few years back salt fish was the main part of the industry (*Narrative Reports* 1966).

In 1969 the same fisheries officer noted that of the 17 fish firms operating in District 37, three were specialised enterprises which were only in business during the lobster season. Between 1961 and 1969 eight year-round plants had either gone out of business or amalgamated with other firms. (There were 22 full-time firms in 1961 as compared with 14 in 1969.) In 1970 several more firms either went out of business or shut down early (*Narrative Reports* 1970). The collapse of groundfish stocks forced the marginal processing enterprises out of business and closed down viable operations until conditions had improved.

During the mid '70s the stocks and the processing sector recovered, but the processing sector emerged from the crisis with a new look and a new orientation. Many of the remaining firms adopted automated processing equipment, such as filleting, deboning, skinning, and heading machines. Also, this decade saw the widespread introduction of plant freezers and coolers. The commitment to fresh and fresh-frozen fish was complete. By the summer of 1984 ten year-round fish plants remained in operation. One of these was a reduction plant that obtained its raw material from the other enterprises. Several of these plants were specialised filleting operations that turned their entire product over to either the Digby Town branch of National Sea Products or Comeau Seafoods, a large, independently owned company based in Saulnierville. In essence they were branches of these larger firms, no longer independent operations that controlled decision-making, marketing and so on. However, the majority of the nine fish buying enterprises remained independent, family-owned businesses. While these plants were more diversified, producing salt fish, fresh fish, and, in several instances, smoked fish, as well as herring products, they also had come to rely heavily upon the production of fresh and frozen fish fillets. A number of these plants also bought and sold lobsters.

Connections Between Draggers and Processors

Fish processing has undergone structural changes of similar magnitude to those experienced by the fish catching sector. The contemporary Digby Neck and the Islands fish plant is the outcome of a consolidation/concentration process that has its origins in the mid to late '50s. Today most of these businesses employ over 40 people during their peak periods, several occasionally employ over 100. With few exceptions, their product lines are specialised and, to some extent, use automated production and sophisticated in-frastructural technologies. The few specialised filleting plants supplying products to the large and economically dominant fish companies represent a significant, recent consolidation in the industry. They may symbolise a major path of future organisational and ownership/control development in the fish processing sector. In fact, the remaining independent Digby Neck and Islands processors report increasing pressure from the large companies, especially National Sea Products. As one processor asserted:

> If I want to stay independent I got to compete with National Sea Products who are competing with me with tax payers money. It makes me mad! If I don't sell 'em all my product they won't deal with me. I called 'em [National Sea, Digby] one day, wanted him to take a load of codfish we had coming in. The son of a bitch wouldn't take 'em. He had the ability to take 'em. Almost wanted them. But he wouldn't take 'em because I wouldn't make a commitment to sell 'em all my fish in the future. They got the markets, they got the money and they're makin' it harder every day for us small companies to stay in it.

Without question, change in the processing sector has been systemically connected with the processes contributing to the transformation of the fish catching sector. As noted earlier, fish buyers /processors and fishers/captains have a history of socio-economic relations in which the former occupy a debt-obligation position to the latter. The fish buyers/processors outfit the fishers/captains, as well as providing them with access to crucial resources such as fuel, frozen bait, coolers and the like. Consequently, most fishers, including those who own their boats and equipment, find themselves in the position of being price-takers, unable to negotiate on fish prices. In this manner, fish buyers as price-givers and debt-obligation holders are able to assure themselves of the consolidated supply produced by many independently owned boats.[1] Supplementing this relationship, fish buyers have often participated in fish supply through direct ownership of boats and equipment. There are two major benefits accruing to buyers from boat ownership. On the one hand, they assure the provision of at least some supply, thereby countering the inherent insecurity of always having to do business with those in control of fish catching capacity. On the other hand, boat ownership provides buyers/processors with a means to control fish prices and, therefore, costs. Through owning boats fish buyers can resist pressure from independent fishers to increase fish prices since they guarantee themselves at least a minimum level of supply. Independent fishers are aware of this and, as a consequence, can be compelled to accept the prices given by fish buyers. Without total control of supply, independent fishers are denied a potentially powerful lever in price negotiations. Thus, it becomes unnecessary for buyers to own a large number of the boats.

This was the case in Digby Neck and the Islands through the late '50s and early '60s. With the movement towards small boat fish draggers, and their demonstrated productivity, a small number of buyers/processors began to play a much larger role in accelerating the acquisition of this catching technology. Dealing with independent owners of mobile, large volume fish producing vessels carries with it different implications and vulnerabilities than buying fish from many hook and line, coastal zone fishing operations. Control of volume supply provided captains/owners with a significant price negotiation lever: a means to undercut the price giving position of fish buyers. Recognising this, several fish buyers were directly, through outright ownership, and indirectly, through financing agreements with fishers, participating in the acquisition of fish draggers by the late '50s. In this manner they were able to secure their position as well as tap into increased supplies of groundfish, especially haddock.

Buyers/processors were able to accomplish this because dismal fish prices and the low incomes associated with fishers' price-taking position had made it almost impossible for fishers to finance dragger acquisitions themselves.[2] In fact, the old tried and true debt-obligation relations between processors and fishers were simply accentuated. Through the '50s fishers gained access to various government sponsored boat and equipment acquisition financing arrangements. These programmes were part of the new modernisation and development thrust that at this time obsessed government and industry. Although ostensibly designed to provide opportunity for fishers, these programmes, of which more detail will be given later, provided only part of the necessary financing. The balance was to be supplied by the fishers through private means, such as bank financing and savings. Given the prevailing fish prices and the resulting low incomes, most had neither the savings nor the capital assets to satisfy their portion of the acquisition costs. Consequently a fishers' access to government financing programmes was usually contingent upon arrangements such as loans from fish buyers, sometimes leaving the buyers with a minority ownership position in the boat purchased. Often buyers co-signed the loans that fishers negotiated with banks. In negotiating loans, fishers often had to provide letters of reference from fish buyers. Thus, in order to take advantage of federal and provincial low interest loan and subsidy

Photo: Fish stages/houses in Westport at low tide
Credit: Anthony Davis

Photo: Cape Island type small boat returning from long lining with catch
Credit: Anthony Davis

programmes for the acquisition of boats and equipment, fishers often had to intensify their debt-obligation relation with fish buyers. Fishers remained price-takers; fish buyers remained price-givers. There were two primary differences between the situation surrounding dragger acquisitions and the circumstances common to the hook and line small boat fisheries: (1) many of the fishers who moved into draggers now worked their boats under a much larger capital debt load then was earlier the case, and (2) fish buyers were much more directly involved in boat acquisitions as minority and sometimes majority owners. These developments enhanced the ability of buyers, especially those moving into fresh fish product lines dependent upon large volume supplies, to sustain their positions as debt-obligation holders and, consequently, as price-givers.

These practices have remained common in the Digby Neck and the Islands fishery; indeed, direct fish buyer/processor participation in the dragger fleet through outright ownership has, if anything, increased since the '60s. Every major fish processor currently in operation owns at least one small boat dragger. Many own two or more of these types of boats while also holding minority positions in other vessels. Since fish processing operations are not given access to government vessel acquisition programmes, this is accomplished through establishing independent boat companies. When asked what advantage accrued to them through boat ownership, most of the seven buyers interviewed replied that guaranteed supply was the primary reason they invested in draggers. In addition to this there are other advantages. As one argued:

> Owning boats gives us both continuity and assurance in our fish supplies. To begin with, this way we're guaranteed that our plant will have supply. But, this also lets us get involved in planning supply. We can direct the captains to fish for certain fish; we can space fishing effort so that we don't find ourselves in a situation of too much oversupply or undersupply. By the way, owning boats also lets us have some control over the quality of fish landed. We insist that our captains take plenty of ice and that they ice the fish properly.

The crews who work these boats receive shares of each trip's catch value after the processor has taken at least 45 percent as a boat share. The percentage will reach as high as 60 percent if the processor pays operating expenses such as fuel. These plants resemble the larger fish processing corporations in that they are in part integrated operations, although small in scale.

In addition to ownership participation, most of the contemporary fish buyers/processors have sustained credit/debt relations with "independent" dragger captains/owners, in both an economic and social sense. *All* of the fish buyers dealing with independently owned draggers acknowledged that they currently provide credit, manage operating expense accounts, and, on occasion, provide personal loans to "their fishers." Perhaps even more importantly, these buyers /processors noted that they frequently assist in fishers' pursuit of fishing licences, bank loans and government financial support. The buyers/processors interviewed reported that the form of assistance provided ranges from helping fishers in the application process (e.g., writing applications and organising submissions) through provision of references in support of applications, to written and personal representations made directly to government officials, bank managers and politicians on the behalf of fishers. These services, frequently referred to as "favours" by buyers/processors, underwrite the creation and maintenance of social/personal debt in relations between buyers/processors and independent captains/owners. That is, fishers assume a situation of obligation as a consequence of favours received; they have to be loyal in selling fish to the buyer/processor providing favours. As one captain expressed it:

> It wouldn't be right, me sellin' to other buyers, at least not right now. He helped me out, helped me get started in drag fishin'. I owe him my fish, at least for awhile. It's the only fair thing to do.

The relation between the growth of the small boat dragger fleet and the fish processors' assumption of an increasing equity position in vessels, as well as their other involvements, mirrors several fundamental shifts in product lines and markets. Salt fish markets for the Atlantic Canadian fishery suffered a major down turn, if not collapse, during the late '50s and early '60s (Alexander 1977). At the same time many processors in southwest Nova Scotia had started to diversify extensively into fresh and frozen fish products. Their proximity and ease of access to the northeastern United States market enabled them, before most others, to participate quickly and fully in the provision of fresh and frozen fish. However, increasing participation and reliance on fresh fish markets brought with it different production requirements. Participation in fresh fish markets usually involved contracts and obligations with Canadian and US buyers which had to be satisfied on time, quickly and regularly. Moreover, participation in these markets required a greater emphasis upon increasing capitalisation of fish plants in the form of processing machinery (e.g., filleting and skinning machines) and freezers/coolers. Volume output was needed to pay for, as well as to utilise, such expanded capacity. Needless to say, the development of small boat dragger technology was ideally suited to, indeed accentuated by, the supply needs of the modernised fish plants in Digby Neck and the Islands. For instance, *all* of the buyers/processors interviewed for this study reported that frozen fish fillets constituted between 51 and 74 per cent of their total fish production, representing a large investment in the machines and plant necessary to produce that particular product. Only substantial, relatively secure levels of resource supply, such as those provided by the small boat fish dragger, can satisfy the demands of such a commitment. The specific interests of the processing sector were, and remain, wedded to the maintenance and future development of the small boat dragger fleet.

The relation between small boat fish draggers and fresh fish, particularly fillet, product lines in the processing sector indicates an interdependence involving increased capital commitments and specialisation. Ironically, both sectors have become increasingly vulnerable to the vagaries of the market, short-falls in the availability of preferred fish species, and the imperatives of the large corporate sector, as a consequence of their interdependence. For instance, the recent declines in groundfish landings have compelled processors to buy increasing amounts from other sources, especially from fish buyers and, in some cases, fishers, in Cape Breton and Newfoundland. Digby Neck and the Islands processors were trucking in substantial supplies of groundfish throughout the summer of 1984, during the time of the year when they normally experienced optimum supply and peak production. This clearly indicates the current extent and the potential seriousness of the problem. Moreover, unlike the situation during the stock collapse of the late '60s and early '70s, when the inshore line fleet provided an alternate supply, this fleet had been so thoroughly reduced by the early '80s that processors could no longer rely on it to compensate for some of their supply shortfalls from draggers.

The only species in abundant supply during the summer of 1984 was pollock. Since pollock is limited in its fresh market appeal, processors lowered the prices as a mechanism to compel dragger captains to reduce their effort on this stock and give more attention to catching other groundfish species, particularly cod and haddock. But locally available cod and haddock stocks have been decimated. The situation is so extreme that many Digby Neck and the Islands draggers have been fishing frequently out of ports in Shelburne and Yarmouth counties over the last couple of years. Captains feel this is necessary in order for them to gain affordable access to exploitable stocks on Browns Bank, as well as on eastern grounds such as LaHave, Sable Island Banks, and those off Cape Breton Island. To the fishers commuting has meant longer time away from home and greater expenses. To the processors this has meant increased transportation and handling costs, as well as concern over the quality of the supply because of the increased length of time it takes for the fish to reach the plant for processing. Several dragger captains insist that the condition of cod and haddock stocks is so bad that boats are increasingly exploiting underaged, small fish. As one claimed:

> There's nothin' here and ya even can't get much on Browns and around except dogfish. A lot of 'em have started fishin' farther to the eastward. They're catchin' a lot of trash [small fish]. They pick out that which can be sold and shovel the rest over the side. These are the fish that would've grown into stock. I'm tellin' ya that things don't look too good for the future.

Several independent owners of small boat draggers report that they have had such poor catches over the last couple of years that it has been a struggle to pay operating costs, let alone generate sufficient income to cover their tremendous capital debts. A few stand to lose their boats to the provincial government's Fishermen's Loan Board as a consequence of failure to meet loan repayment schedules. Some fishers insisted that a number of processors are buying up re-claimed boats for an extremely low price, reaping advantage from the fishers' pitiful situation. While the fishers argue that processors should not be permitted to buy boats, the processors are now so dependent upon dragger supply that they have few options remaining, particularly since the line fishery has ceased to be significant. The Digby Neck and the Islands fishery appears to face a Catch-22 dilemma. To a large extent, the current crisis has been brought on by the coupling of small boat dragger technology with the consolidation and capitalisation of fish processing. Processor dependence upon this system of production has developed to the extent that in order to survive the crisis they feel compelled to intensify their dependence.

Photo: East Ferry fish plant with two small boat draggers at wharf.
Credit: Anthony Davis

Government Interventions: The Drive to Industrialise the Fisheries

7

THE PUSH TO INDUSTRIALISE

While small boat drag net fishing in Digby Neck and the Islands began independently of the government, its full-fledged development as an efficient volume production fishing technology, wedded to the modernisation of fish processing, was encouraged by federal and provincial policies designed to accelerate the industrialisation of the fisheries.[1] As noted earlier, producers and processors had lobbied the federal government to place a freeze on the application of large dragger technology, in effect, barring its development in the Atlantic Canadian fishing industry. World War II changed all this. The push to increase overall food production, as one dimension of the war effort, spilled over into the Atlantic Canadian fishing industry. Government saw the east coast fishery as inefficient and archaic, in need of an industrialisation, modernisation push:

> The Fisheries Department wasted no time in reorienting its policy to rectify the inefficiencies and short-falls of the east coast fishery... With the appointment of Ernest Bertrand (Laurier) as Minister of Fisheries in 1942, the modernization policy mushroomed with subsidies for dragger construction and schooner conversion to trawling gear. Such offshore development programmes were supplemented by government sponsorship of an experimental inshore boat design—the longliner. The intent of these programmes was to upgrade the efficiency of both the independent producer and the corporate fishery... Steward Bates' *Report on the Atlantic Sea-Fishery* for the Nova Scotia Royal Commission on Provincial Development and Rehabilitation marked the call-to-arms for the province. His analysis was essentially that underdevelopment in the fishing industry was the legacy of regulations such as the trawler restrictions of the 1930s, and chronically undercapitalized

primary and secondary production. With the growing prospects of substantial federal transfer funds to underwrite their activities, the province created the Fisheries Division of the Department of Trade and Industry to deal with the dual problem of encouraging large-scale development, and re-equipping smaller-scale fishermen (Barrett 1984:79).

These developments threw open the doors to the industrialisation of the fisheries, a process directly aided by government financial assistance and policy. While this process began during the war, the modernisation push actually picked up momentum during the next two decades:

> The [Nova Scotia] Fisheries Loan Board, with federal assistance, launched a subsidy program for independently owned, medium-sized longliners and draggers. Between 1947 and 1960, 125 longliners and 34 draggers were built in Nova Scotia with such assistance. Federal subsidies for larger vessel construction averaged $7,732 per vessel between 1947 and 1965, a period in which approximately 32 vessels were added to the Nova Scotian fleet. A notable regulation passed in 1953 made federal subsidies contingent upon the affiliation of large trawlers with processing companies (Barrett 1984:79).

The explosive growth of the Digby Neck and the Islands small boat dragger fleet during the late '50s and early '60s was triggered by these programmes. This technology and its potentials dove-tailed with the federal and provincial governments' imperative to modernise and industrialise the industry. A 1970 federally commissioned study on the impact and utility of government vessel construction/equipment purchase loan and subsidy programmes argued that these programmes had contributed successfully to the upgrading of fishing capacity and productivity (Mitchell and Frick 1970). Of particular relevance in this analysis are the authors' remarks concerning the impact of government financial aid programmes upon the intermediate-sized fleet, the category of vessels containing small boat draggers:

> Although it is difficult to assess the economic performance of vessels...it has been found that intermediate-sized vessels are capable of realizing adequate returns on investment...From recent studies on returns to large trawlers of 100 gross tons and over it seems that intermediate-sized vessels rank as the most efficient vessels in the offshore fleet on the Atlantic Coast...The subsidy program at the outset, by covering vessels from 55 to 65 feet, therefore promoted a desirable size of vessel (Mitchell and Frick 1970:50).

Between 1956 and 1964, federal and provincial governments provided an average of 84 percent of the financing (17 percent through federal boat construction assistance and 67 percent through provincial loan boards) for Atlantic Canadians purchasing 50 to 60 foot fish draggers, which at that time cost around $50,000.[2] As a cash downpayment, fishers provided only about 16 percent of the purchase price. But this portion represented, on average, $8,372, a substantial sum given the questionable ability of producers either to generate surplus income or to develop equity in a dismal fish price environment. As would be expected, many Digby Neck and the Islands fishers report that in order to cover their end of the purchase they had to obtain assistance from fish buyers in forms such as co-signed bank loans, outright cash contributions and letters of reference for lending institutions. Government programmes, while providing some fishers with access to the means to modernise and industrialise their fishing capacity, actually perpetuated and, in many instances, deepened producer dependence and obligation to fish buyers/processors. The large loan component of government assistance saddled individual fishers with a tremendous debt burden, the enormity of which motivated many to increase their fishing efforts dramatically. This could only have negative impacts upon fish stocks and upon relations between fishers employing different technologies. Indeed, the much remarked upon conflict in the Atlantic Canadian fishing industry between those employing different technologies can be argued to have been exacerbated by this form of government intervention.[3]

Regardless of the consequences, these government programmes accelerated the transformation of fishing efforts. For instance, by 1968–69, the federal vessel construction assistance programme had aided in the construction and acquisition of 285 vessels falling between 25 and 99.9 gross tons in Nova Scotia alone (Mitchell and Frick 1970:39). Many of these were small boat fish draggers. Alterations in government loan and subsidy programmes during 1964–65 extended assistance to fishers purchasing boats down to 35 feet in length and under 25 gross tons. For the first time coastal zone fishers were permitted ready access to financing programmes. Between 1965 and 1968, 192 Nova Scotian boat purchases were assisted under this programme (Mitchell and Frick 1970:39). The economists appraising the various governmental boat acquisition assistance initiatives were very critical of the changes that provided coastal zone fishers with access to the programmes.

> Only small numbers of ... inshore craft were subsidized under the Department of Fisheries program when the minimum length of

vessels eligible was 45 feet. The inclusion in the program in 1964 of 'experimental' vessels down to 35 feet minimum length opened the flood gates, however; the term 'experimental' was liberally interpreted in practice and the provincial boards responsible for administering the program lost control. However, the main criticism would be levelled against the federal government authorities for introducing the amendment without due regard to its probable consequences and its incompatibility with the basic objectives of the Department's subsidy program (Mitchell and Frick 1970:35).

The industrialisation/modernisation focus of governmental assistance to the fishery is revealed in these statements. While boat construction assistance was restricted to intermediate and large-sized vessels, the programmes were considered consistent with their intended purpose, that is, to aid in the development of a modern, rationalised Atlantic Canadian fishing industry. Coastal zone fishers and their communities did not fit into this image. They were considered the purveyors of an archaic and economically inefficient form of production:

> By encouraging an increase in the number of inshore vessels the subsidy program contributed to the perpetuation and exacerbation of problems in the inshore fisheries. This is considered to be the major short-coming of the program...The subsidy program, in so far as it facilitated the movement of inshore fishermen to offshore fishing by the use of larger vessels, has been beneficial (Mitchell and Frick 1970:50–51).

The consequences of development programmes, such as boat construction assistance, upon community life and the ability of fishers to pursue successfully their chosen livelihoods, did not receive any studied consideration. These dimensions of the industry were viewed as secondary to the requirements for an "economic" industry, that is, an industry championing increasing capitalisation of production, consolidation of production efforts and the industrialisation of work processes. While perhaps delayed by a number of unforeseen circumstances, these objectives appear to have been nearly realised in the Digby Neck and the Islands fisheries.

Government programmes targeted on modernising fish production were coupled with like initiatives directed at the processing sector:

> The expansion of Atlantic Coast processing capacity was encouraged by provincial and federal government assistance in various forms, and plant expansion and fleet expansion were mutually reinforcing; new plant capacity needed the assurance of a large and continual supply of fish; loan and subsidy assistance

for the construction of fishing vessels made these easier to obtain, while new processing capacity ensured a port market for the catch of the additional vessels (Mitchell and Frick 1970:52).

Without question the systemic relation between the development of the Digby Neck and the Islands small boat dragger fleet and the re-orientation of fish processing was facilitated through these forms of governmental intervention. Fish processing on Digby Neck and the Islands underwent consolidation and reorganization throughout the '60s. A few new, highly capitalised plants employing fish processing machinery and refrigeration technology replaced many salt-fish producing operations. Salt fish gave way to the production of fresh and frozen products, a re-orientation tied to the sort of year-round, volume fish production associated with small boat draggers.

Governmental Management of Access and Participation

Ironically, completion of the industrialisation design was short-circuited by collapse of North Atlantic groundfish stocks in the late '60s to early '70s. This collapse is directly attributable to the over-exploitation of stocks by foreign and Canadian fish draggers. As we have seen in an earlier section, this resulted in a temporary reduction in the Digby Neck and the Islands dragger fleet as well as fishing effort. At this time sufficient coastal zone, especially hook and line, fishing capacity remained able to compensate partially for decreases in dragger landings. These events constitute a hiatus on the road of rational fisheries development.

Stock collapse created an industry crisis which compelled government to de-emphasise industrial development and focus upon the creation of stock and access management strategies. The central problem of the industry was redefined as too much capacity uncontrollably pursuing too few fish. Consequently, the federal government developed policies intended to interface fishing effort with the biological capacity of stocks to bear specific rates of exploitation.[4]

> The groundfish crisis of 1974 ... led to an intensive review of fisheries policy which culminated in the Commercial Fisheries policy of 1976. In this document the Canadian government set the management objective for fisheries as being 'best use' or optimum sustained yield (OSY) which implicitly recognized OSY as being a dynamic ESY [economic sustained yield], also taking into account various intangibles such as social factors. MSY [maximum sustained yield] was discarded (Macdonald 1984:29).

Forced by the collapse of groundfish stocks to shift away from the modernisation thrust, federal policy began to focus on putting in place mechanisms that controlled access to marine resources. In short, the fundamental problem facing the development of the industry was redefined. The argument for modernisation through the adoption of new and better technologies was replaced by a biologically-grounded perspective that insisted the industry had too many fishers pursuing too few fish. The proposed solution was the development of a more refined, sophisticated and comprehensive management and regulation regime to limit and control access to marine resources through mechanisms such as licences and quotas. With this change, government placed a much greater emphasis on policing fish catching and processing activities in order to assure compliance with the new regime of regulations (Macdonald 1984:29). By the late '70s, commitment to this approach of fisheries management had become thoroughly entrenched. Now the thrust of government policy was to regulate precisely the exploitation of marine resources by making participation in specific fisheries with particular technologies contingent upon the annual provision of government issued licences.

The extent and character of this strategy is evident in Table 11, which profiles the number of licences issued by the federal government in Digby Neck and the Islands (Fisheries District 37) for specific fisheries between 1963 and 1983. In 1963 participation in only four of the fisheries presented was contingent upon fishers obtaining licences. By 1983 participation in every fishery, with the exception of handline fishing, had become tied to a licence. While echoes of the licence management approach are evident through the '60s, its full realisation becomes apparent only after the stock collapse. Notably, the declaration of the 200 mile economic management zone in January 1977 added further impetus to the government's commitment to management through licensing.

THE CONSEQUENCES OF LIMITED ENTRY MANAGEMENT

This management approach has elicited, in many instances, a response from fishers which contradicts the purpose of the licensing programme. When licences for specific fisheries were introduced, many fishers without a history of participation in these fisheries obtained licences. This is demonstrated in Table 11. For example, groundfish entry permits for otter trawl were introduced during 1977–78. In 1979, 69 permits for otter trawl were issued to Digby Neck and the Islands fishers. As previous data reveal, the number of licences dispensed far surpassed the actual number of vessels participating in the otter trawl groundfisheries. In 1979, there were a total of 24 small boat draggers fishing out of Digby Neck and

Photo: Nets, lobster traps, fish sheds along the Tiverton shore road
Credit: Anthony Davis

TABLE 11: Number of Fishing Licences Issued by Selected Specific Fisheries, Digby Neck and the Islands (District 37), 1963-1983[1]

Specific Fisheries[2]	Year[3]																		
	1963	1964	1965	1966	1967	1968	1969	1970	1971	1972	1973	1974	1977	1978	1979	1980	1981	1982	1983
LOBSTER[4]																			
Undifferentiated	300	355	342	382	340	-	-	-	-	-	-	-	-	-	-	-	-	-	-
Operator	-	-	-	-	-	157	208	202	203	195	188	185	129	126	123	116	107	98	94
Part-time/Helper	-	-	-	-	-	179	-	-	-	-	-	-	-	-	-	-	-	-	-
SCALLOP	N/A	N/A	N/A	N/A	N/A	4	3	1	1	N/A	3	2	2	5	6	9	12	14	11
HERRING																			
Weir	20	14	11	11	13	16	21	20	17	20	20	19	20	19	19	N/A	N/A	N/A	N/A
Undifferentiated	-	-	-	-	-	-	-	-	-	-	-	-	-	-	-	-	-	-	-
Gill Net	-	-	-	-	-	-	-	-	-	-	39	32	32	-	-	-	-	-	-
Drift Gill Net	-	-	-	-	-	-	-	-	-	-	-	-	20	17	17	N/A	19	19	21
Set Gill Net	-	-	-	-	-	-	-	-	-	-	-	-	-	93	95	N/A	109	89	86
Carriers/Pumpers	-	-	-	-	-	-	-	-	-	-	3	3	-	8	8	12	8	9	6
GROUNDFISH																			
Otter Trawl	23	25	27	25	21	20	21	22	20	16	14	18	6	43	69	47	42	42	42
Longline	-	-	-	-	-	-	-	-	-	-	-	-	21	52	80	104	101	92	90

Source: Department of Fisheries and Oceans, Statistics Division.

1. Data for the period 1963-78 only include licences issued by fisheries officers in District 37. The post 1978 data include all licences issued for District 37. The Digby Town office of DFO could have issued additional licences. These data do not include the personal fishermen's licence required for all fishermen.

2. Not all fisheries requiring licences are presented here. For instance, licences for Groundfish Gill Nets first appeared in the data in 1977, Midwater Herring Trawl in 1980, Squid Otter Trawl in 1980, Shrimp licences in 1981, Swordfish Harpoon in 1981, Mackerel Purse Seine in 1981, Groundfish Danish in 1982, Groundfish Scottish in 1982, Squid Jigging in 1982, and Mackerel Set Gill Net in 1982. While not many of these and other types of licences were issued for Digby Neck fishermen, their proliferation since 1977 clearly indicates the management orientation of the federal government—an orientation emphasising strict control of access and participation through licensing.

3. Data for 1975 and 1976 were not available.

4. Trap limits, trap tags and other lobster fishery requirements were introduced in 1968. Special licences for helpers were only issued on a widespread basis for the 1968 season. Moreover, these data do not differentiate license 'classes.' That is, they do not distinguish class 'A' (full-time) from Class 'B' (part-time) licences. The former permits holders to fish up to the maximum number of allowable traps (375) while the latter restricts holders to fishing no more than 250 traps.

5. After 1976 licences to participate in the groundfishery are referred to as Groundfish Entry Permits. Only handline fishing does not require a specific licence. The low number of licences issued in 1977 may be the result of confusion resulting from the period of transition between licensing systems.

Islands ports. Realising that this situation contravened the limited entry management purpose of licences, the Department of Fisheries and Oceans attached conditions to licence renewal. Captains could only renew their otter trawl permit if they either were demonstrably preparing to use the licence or were actually participating in the fishery. Several fishers responded by entering the fishery. In part, this explains the six boat increase in the number of draggers working out of Digby Neck and the Islands ports between 1979 and 1980 (see Table 9). This constituted a 25 percent increase in dragger fishing effort over one year. As one dragger captain who reacted this way explained:

> It was either go into it or lose my licence. I'd been thinkin' about doin' it anyway. Things looked good. You could make some money at it then. So, I made the jump. Could say I was sort of pushed I suppose.

Of course this resulted in dramatically increased fishing capacity and fishing effort in the dragger sector.

Other fishers responded to licence renewal conditions by purchasing some of the equipment associated with drag net fishing. In this manner they created the illusion of pending participation and, therefore, retained their licences. One such captain outlined his motives in this way:

> They told me that unless I used the licence I was goin' to lose it. So, I went out and bought part of a drag net, rollers, some netting. It's all layin' out in the shed. It cost me somethin' but I still got my licence. Had to do it. What happens if nothin's goin' in line or lobster fishin'? I might just have to get into it. Gotta make a livin' some how. I knew if they took it away I'd never see it again. So I spent the money to keep the licence. They [DFO] make ya do things this way.

Some captains are convinced that in order to make a living at fishing they have to retain as much flexibility in their options as possible. In short, they believe that success in the small boat fishing business is contingent upon their ability to switch from one fishery and technological approach to others, depending upon what seems to be the most appropriate strategy for exploiting available resources. But diversified effort flies in the face of the federal government's limited entry licence approach to fisheries management. This approach pivots on the idea of controlling fishing effort by restricting entry, a management strategy that produces specialists.[5]

In addition to creating specialists, management through limited entry licensing has contradicted and eroded producer-developed, local-level, informal systems of proprietorship and access management. As described in Chapter 3, coastal zone fishers from each community in the region historically worked within a set of informal rules concerning who fishes where and how fishing should be conducted (e.g., types and quantities of gear to be used, courtesies to be followed and so on). Fishers arrived at these rules through years of experience, reflecting a consensual and, therefore, co-operative approach to the management of and participation in ocean resource exploitation. The consensual and co-operative aspects of local-level rules are fundamental to the fishers' notion of proprietorship, as is reflected in the cognitive designation of defined coastal zones as "our ground," meaning the fishing ground of the people from this wharf and this community. Moreover, local-level rules of access and use reflect the widely held principle that *all* fishers working out of the same harbour and community have an equal need and right to access resources in order to make their living, especially where generations of persons from the same families have fished a ground continuously. The rules express the complementary principle that individual behaviours jeopardizing the livelihood goals of many will not be countenanced. In short, the small boat coastal fishers' notion of proprietorship expresses a co-operative common stake/common situation/common background rationality (see endnote 2, Chapter 3).

In contrast to the small boat fishers' sense of proprietorship, the federal government expresses its constitutionally legitimated proprietorship over ocean territory through granting *individuals* the *privilege* of access to ocean resources through licensing, as long as licence holders adhere to the specifications of their licences, for example, species fished and quantity and type of gear used. This approach expresses the assumption that, prior to government intervention, the fisheries were characterised by the competitive anarchy of self-seeking, maximising individuals bent on taking as much resource as possible for themselves, before their competitors (all other fishers) could get it. In this approach there is little, if any, knowledge of or sensitivity to local-level notions of proprietorship, common stake and access management. Consequently, the government's limited entry licensing policy, said to be necessary for the good of the industry as well as the economic conditions of fishers, collided with and contradicted local-level, consensual and co-operative modes of behaviour and organisation. With the power of sanctions at hand, the government compelled compliance and, in so doing, engaged in a form of intervention that fuelled conflict between itself and fishers. The individualist, self-seeking, maximiser rationality embedded in limited entry licensing has become, to an extent, prophecy fulfilled in so far as many fishers, especially the ones benefiting from possession of licences, see little utility in adhering to local-level rules. After all, the federal government, not the local fraternity of fishers, exercises ultimate authority and power over the conditions of access and participation. Those in possession of licences have their privileges assured; all others must obtain possession in order to participate—particularly as captain/boat owners. Within such conditions, it is little wonder that local-level occupational solidarities become less relevant to participation, and conflict comes to occupy a more prominent position in fisher-government as well as fisher-fisher relations.

Another consequence of limited entry licensing is seen in the development of new types of formalised inequity within the small boat fisheries. That is, those in possession of licences, especially licences permitting access to high value resources such as lobster, shrimp and crab and high volume technologies such as the otter trawl, occupy an advantaged socio-economic position relative to the situation of other fishers. This advantage expresses itself in a number of ways. To begin with, possessors of high value/high volume licences are permitted exclusive participation in fisheries that ordinarily provide substantial incomes. Secondly, limits on the numbers of licences available creates a circumstance of scarcity relative to demand. Aside from inventing a market in licences that hithertofore had not existed, this situation creates and fuels inflation in the selling prices of licences. For example, the cost of obtaining a lobster licence in Nova Scotia commonly ranges between $35,000 and $65,000, depending upon the lobster district within which it can be fished. Prices such as those are prohibitive for many current, full-time participants, particularly crew.

The distributional features of fishers' incomes in southwest Nova Scotia illustrate this condition. A study of 1981 income data revealed the average *net income* of southwest Nova Scotian coastal zone captains (N=62) to be $11,066, while that of crew (N=26) stood at $9,356 (unpublished analysis by Davis and Thiessen). In the lobster fishery alone, a more recent study (1988) revealed that captains *netted* an average of $38,841 while crew earned $10,447. This latter income distribution characterises a fishery where the purchase costs of a new boat and lobster traps are reported, in the same study, to range between $72,000 and $118,000, not including the cost of the licence—an additional expense of around $50,000 (The Scotia-Fundy Lobster Fishery Working Committee 1989:67). Given these income data, under what conditions can full-time crew realistically aspire to boat ownership, captaincy and participation in the economically important lobster fishery? Similar conditions pertain in the independent captain/owner sector of the southwest Nova Scotia offshore fishery, which includes most vessels in the small boat dragger sector. In this instance, the unpublished study of 1981 income data revealed that offshore captains/owners (N=22) made an average net income of $73,076 while crew (N=44) reported an average net income of $18,998. A companion, published study revealed that enterprise market values in offshore fisheries such as otter trawl, lobster and purse seine were well in excess of $100,000, not including the value of the licences (Thiessen and Davis 1988).

While licence holders realise profound economic advantages from the government-issued privilege to fish, many of those without licences but committed to and dependent upon the fisheries for their livelihoods are effectively barred from ever obtaining licences by the artificially-inflated cost. Increasingly, fishers without licences are destined to a life of lower-income returns, frequently earned by working in someone else's boat. Finally, the limited entry licensing programme provides the children of high income licence holders with enhanced access to possession and participation, through inheritance or intra-familial purchase transfers.[6]

In addition to eroding local-level systems of consensual and co-operative proprietorship, limited entry licensing has put in place the economic conditions and imperatives necessary for the development of extensive social differentiation, creating divisions between small boat fishers within each community. This policy has already been linked to the appearance of concrete class divisions within the small boat fishing fraternity. Some captains/owners of small boat enterprises, once in possession of licences for high income fisheries, have been reported to have used their earnings to purchase additional boats and licences, as well as to invest in fish processing businesses and other ventures, in order to accumulate and reproduce wealth. Within these harbours, fishers without possession of such advantageous permits express anger, resentment and distrust, both in terms of the individuals so benefited and the policy which has created privilege and extended differential advantages (see Sinclair 1983 and Sinclair 1985). The development of significant differences among fishers in the material condition of life are evident in Digby Neck and the Islands communities. Invariably, the newest houses, grand in scale and sporting paved driveways, TV satellite dishes, latest year trucks and cars, and all-terrain vehicles are owned by fishing captains/small boat owners who participate in the drag net and lobster fisheries. Through the course of interviews, a couple of the small boat dragger captains revealed investment holdings in boats, herring weirs and fish plants. As could be expected, fishers not in a similar position expressed strongly-held, negative opinions about the character of some of the advantaged captains. For instance, one such captain was said to have pushed the crew so hard that his success was won with "the taking of more than a few fingers and other serious injuries." Another advantaged captain was described as "a heartless bastard who don't care what it takes as long as his boat is full." Regardless of whether fact or fiction, the attribution of such features to fellow fishers certainly foretells of friction and discontent as a consequence of a developing socio-economic differentiation and, perhaps, the formation of class divisions among Digby Neck and the Islands fishers.

While contributing to the expansion of drag net fishing capacity, as well as compelling some captains to create the illusion of pending participation, the attachment of conditions to licence renewal did reduce the number of permits issued (see Table 11). Between 1981–83 a total of 42 drag net permits were issued, a 39 percent reduction over the number distributed in 1979. The same strategy was employed by the Department of Fisheries and Oceans in terms of regulating access to herring gill net licences and longline groundfish entry permits. In addition, the DFO introduced a lobster licence buy-back programme during the late '70s and early '80s in order to reduce effort in this fishery (see Table 11). Today, many coastal zone fishers are specialists, holding licences that only provide them with access to particular fisheries. Changes to the Unemployment Insurance Regulations, introduced in June 1983, put a seal on this process. These changes provided fishers with the option of drawing unemployment insurance benefits either during the summer season (late spring to mid-fall) or during the winter season (mid-fall to late spring).[7] Throughout Digby Neck and the Islands restricted entry management has helped push the coastal zone fishery into a largely part-time, specialised activity. At the same time, these programmes have directly resulted in the expansion of dragger fishing capacity and therefore increased pressure on declining groundfish stocks. This makes it even more unlikely that coastal zone fishers will be able to break away from specialisation and the concomitant dependence upon governmental income support.[8]

In addition, many of the remaining coastal zone fishers, as well as dragger captains, are currently faced with servicing the large debts resulting from their purchase of boats and equipment at inflated prices. Ironically, federal and provincial vessel acquisition subsidy programmes fuelled increases in the prices of boats. Boat builders and equipment suppliers have been the real beneficiaries of these programmes since they have consistently increased their prices in relation to the level of subsidisation available, leaving the fishers who receive assistance without any real savings. Those who fail to obtain assistance pay a price for boats that is inflated by the level of subsidisation available. Consequently, they pay a double cost and face the requirement of regularly meeting payments on enormous capital debts (Baker 1979). Increased debt, combined with specialisation, contributes to the factors motivating captains to maximise their fishing effort, thereby placing more exploitative pressure on available marine resources and hastening the likelihood of stock collapse.

The dramatic increase since the early '70s in federal and provincial government direct management intervention in the fishing industry has had a predictable impact upon industry relations with government. Almost without exception, contemporary Digby Neck and the Islands fishers and fish processors condemn the substance of government intervention. Government programmes, be they concerned with limited entry, quality enhancement or health standards, are commonly perceived as intended to prohibit, not facilitate, the development of the industry. Of course, criticism is directed at aspects of government intervention that require those affected to bear the dollar and organisational costs of adherence to regulations. Little negative comment is heard about those programmes that enable fishers and processors to pursue their goals successfully.

The sheer number and questionable character of specifications concerning practically every aspect of participation, which are continually dispensed by both levels of government, convinces many that an informed, simplified and co-ordinated approach to management and development assistance is desperately needed. Few argue that government does not have a necessary role in the fishery; to most, the problem concerns the way in which that role has been fulfilled.

Digby Neck and the Islands fishers and independent fish processors are largely convinced that government does not intervene with their interests in mind. For instance, when asked whether or not they think some companies influence government policies, every one of the processors interviewed insisted that the needs and requirements of large corporations such as National Sea Products directly shape the character of the government's involvement. Several went so far as to claim that the large companies directly determine the substance of government intervention. As one processor argued:

> The governments have put so much into companies like National
> Sea that they can't afford to do anything else but keep puttin' more

in. So, the government has got to do what they [the corporations] want. They're tied together. Hell, they can walk into the Minister's office anytime they want. I can't do that. The big companies get what they want.

Regardless of the factual substance in this perspective, it does reflect a commonly held opinion, an opinion which does not enhance relations among fishers, fish processors and various levels of government.

The increased tension between participants in Digby Neck and the Islands' fishing industry and government, as a consequence of management intervention since the early 1970s, was officially remarked upon by District 37 fisheries officers as early as 1974. For instance, one reported that:

Relations with industry appear to be strained more so than in previous years. This is also due to more regulations not only by our own branch but by all Government branches (*Narrative Report* January 1975).

And furthermore:

With more and more restrictions being placed upon the various fisheries re: conservation [sic]...Fishermen of today appear to be more suspicious than in previous years (*Narrative Report* January 1975).

Aside from affecting the atmosphere of industry/government dealings, this fisheries officer noted that strained and suspicious relations made it increasingly difficult for him to gather reliable information, the supposed basis for government policy formation (*Narrative Report* January 1975).

In this chapter I have argued that the federal and provincial governments have facilitated the transformation of the Digby Neck and the Islands fishery from a predominantly coastal zone based activity to a high volume, capitalised industry. In the process, government has provided the means for the dragger fleet to grow and the processing sector to modernise and consolidate. These developments have reduced the coastal zone fishery to a largely seasonal activity that has become increasingly reliant upon government transfers and income supports. Yet relations between government and *all* sectors of the Digby Neck and the Islands industry have become more strained and riven with suspicion. The dilemma of industry dependence upon high volume dragger catches in an era of declining groundfish stocks has been accentuated by the substance of government intervention. Indeed, these outcomes all raise serious questions about the character of and interests reflected in governmental policies.

Photo: Little River small boat, fish houses/stages, and fish floats
Credit: Anthony Davis

Conclusion 8

This volume has described and interpreted socio-economic and ecological conditions characteristic of the contemporary Digby Neck and the Islands fishing industry. Many participants in all sectors of this industry are concerned about its immediate future as well as their ability to satisfy income needs. This situation has come about as a consequence of the relation between the adoption of the small boat fish dragger, the consolidation and capitalisation of fish processing, and the push by governments to facilitate modernisation/industrialisation. The interplay of these three factors has transformed the fishery. Once a low capital debt industry with the flexibility to respond successfully to variations in economic and resource supply conditions, it is now a relatively highly capitalised endeavor that features several largely specialised forms of fish catching and processing. As a consequence many contemporary participants have become increasingly vulnerable to the vagaries of economic and resource supply conditions.

Deriving a livelihood from activities dependent upon regular access to marine resources is often problematic. After all, marine resources are usually undomesticated, frequently mobile, and subject to substantial exploitation pressures. Market returns are uncertain. Consequently, fishers and fish processors who specialise in exploiting a select range of products severely limit their options when access to sufficient resources or to adequate economic returns becomes limited. Compounding such vulnerabilities are the debt burdens that frequently accompany specialisation. Enterprises that specialise often do so through adopting new technologies, that is, through capitalising the operation. The debt associated with financing capitalisation has a primary lien on income generated. Such a situation amplifies the operational vulnerability of fish catching and fish processing enterprises to reduced resource supply and depressed market conditions.

The Digby Neck and the Islands fishing industry currently faces several dilemmas that have their origins in the relation between increasing capitalisation, over-exploitation of resources and specialisation. In dramatically increasing the production of certain groundfish species, the small boat fish dragger has contributed to the over-exploitation of stocks. But dragger captains, confronted with the necessity to satisfy loan payments, have few options other than to continue to increase their exploitative pressure on the reduced fish stocks. Several of the captains who have seen the writing on the wall are currently attempting to sell their draggers in an effort to rescue some of their equity. But the demand for this type of vessel is currently so low that they must either reduce the selling price dramatically and surrender equity or attempt to hang on until conditions improve and, in the process, risk losing all to the provincial Fishermen's Loan Board. Neither of these options offers captains much of a choice, particularly in regard to their future in the industry.

Many processors confront a similar situation. Their enterprises are committed to high volume production of fresh and/or frozen fillets. Needless to say, these types of operations, also the outcome of capitalisation, require the large and consistent volumes of supply produced by fish draggers. Persistent shortfalls delay debt repayment, threaten markets and, eventually, close plants. The future fate of processors is wedded to that of fish draggers. Each requires the other, yet the continuation and consequent worsening of existing conditions can only reduce the ability of any to survive. Further consolidation is the most optimistic outcome of this process.

The data presented show that the coastal zone fishery, once the industry's backbone, has been reduced to a part-time, seasonal and increasingly specialised activity. Both the development of the dragger-processor nexus and the thrust of government management and development practices have contributed to this process. As marginalised producers, coastal zone fishers are now more dependent upon government income supplements than at any time in the past. The imperative expressed in the organisation and management of the fisheries suggests that the coastal zone situation will most likely get much worse before it can improve. Ironically, these circumstances have effectively eliminated the coastal zone, small boat fisheries as a back-up form of production when dragger effort comes up short. This development only deepens processor dependence on dragger supply, thereby accentuating the push for draggers to increase fishing effort. It is probable that a sustained reduction in lobster stocks would push the coastal zone fisheries over the edge, essentially removing it as a significant feature of the Digby Neck and the Islands industry.

As the data concerning population and industry structure indicate, the impact of the industry's development through the past 40 years has been experienced differentially among Digby Neck and Islands communities. Only those few communities associated with the dragger-processor nexus show any vitality. The majority face a future of limited possibilities. As one fisher proclaimed: "All that draggers done around here is make a few millionaires while the rest of us 'ave been left paupers." While such outcomes may be consistent with the overall thrust of government policies to reduce fishing effort and "rationalise" the industry, their impact upon communities, families and livelihoods does not rest comfortably with many of those affected. Nor can it be expected to. After all, their livelihoods, their communities, and their way of life have been jeopardised.

The organisational changes profiled in this volume and their consequences for the ability of human communities to pursue livelihoods of choice, reveal several important aspects of the socio-economic interests and imperatives imbedded in the present structure of the fishing industry. A number of years ago Raoul Andersen, an anthropologist at Memorial University of Newfoundland, argued that qualitative structural changes in the management and organisation of the fishing industry were going to be essential for Atlantic Canadian fishing communities to derive significant benefits from extended jurisdiction (Andersen 1978). To this end, Andersen reasoned that new decision-making processes and access management arrangements, such as mechanisms for fishers, their families and community to determine the priorities of management and the conditions of participation, were crucial if equitable distributions of benefits were to be assured. He argued that anything short of this sort of restructuring would simply amount to "additive change," that is, essentially a continuation of existing organisation, policy direction and control. An outcome such as this was seen as primarily benefiting policy-makers in government offices, the vertically-integrated fish processing firms and a few, advantaged, independent operators (Andersen 1978). Unfortunately, Andersen's concerns have fallen on deaf ears.

While occasionally paying lip service to the so-called "human side" of the industry,[1] government policy has persisted in its intent to rationalise the fishing industry. The late '60s and early '70s collapse of groundfish stocks did convince government managers

that biological and ecological considerations were essential to en-
suring a future for the industry. But rather than identifying the
imperatives and economic logic driving the fishing efforts of highly
capitalised enterprises as central to resource over-exploitation, the
federal government focused its efforts in developing more precise
mechanisms to regulate and police the fishing activities of all
participants. This approach has been disastrous for most, especially
independent catching and processing enterprises economically dependent upon regular access to a variety of resources. Moreover, the
regulatory and policing approach has created an industry-wide
atmosphere of distrust and conflict.[2] Rather than concluding that
the fundamental problem facing the industry was too many enterprises chasing too few fish, government policy-makers should have
recognised that certain types of fishing enterprises, such as drag
and seine boats, especially when coupled with the economic interests of fish processors, exert much more exploitative pressure on
fish stocks than other sorts of enterprises. The highly capitalised
ventures necessarily, and predictably, must claim a disproportionate share of available resources. When they are either owned by
or economically tied to fish processing operations that are equally
developed as capital-intensive ventures, high volume production
enterprises receive an added push to maximise fishing effort.[3] Such
basic economic conditions alone would predispose enterprises, if
unfettered, to over-exploit fish stocks. These conditions, coupled
with goals to maximise income and accumulate profits, create a
capitalised sector that is driven to extract as much as possible from
the resource base. Such a combination can only bring calamity for
most of the people and communities dependent upon the industry.
Government managers have yet to develop policies that seriously
come to grips with this circumstance. The quota, licensing and
policing strategies do little but entrench the situation by defining a
disproportionate share of fish stocks as the rightful property of the
capitalised sector. Management strategies that direct highly
capitalised fishing and processing enterprises to exploit stocks that
are geographically or seasonally inaccessible to the coastal zone and
small boat sector would be much more supportive of creating an
economically self-sustaining industry—one which responds to the
needs and priorities of the majority of those dependent upon it.

The transformations and the resulting structural dilemmas
within the Digby Neck and the Islands fisheries express fundamental
characteristics of the form and dynamics of the region's social
structure and social relations. These social characteristics and
dynamics constitute the medium in and through which the trans-

formations have taken place, thereby giving them their current shape and substance. While this volume has been concerned mainly with charting the broad currents and primary players in these changes and dilemmas within the Digby Neck and Islands fishery, the prevailing social structure and the general ways in which it has conditioned the region's social and economic responses and outcomes have been sketched out. The information and analyses presented have shown that those fish buyers/processors who were quick off the mark in recognising the benefits of the small boat dragger, encouraged and participated in its adoption, often assuming at least a partial ownership position. In this manner these buyers/processors were able to sustain and reproduce their position of economic power and dominance vis-à-vis fishers and in particular, vis-à-vis dragger captains/owners and the fisheries dependent communities on Digby Neck and the Islands. The two most prominent remaining independent fish firms have risen to their current position as a direct consequence of acquiring dragger technology, striking special relationships with independent dragger captains/owners, and developing processing capacity for mechanised fresh and frozen fish production.[4]

The ties between these fish processors and dragger captains/owners are particularly illustrative of the sorts of social relationships which arise as a vehicle for the pursuit of vested interests, and are both symptomatic of and purveyors of the dynamics and outcomes that have been discussed. Even in an economic environment of low fish prices and credit-debt relationships, fishers and their families express, within their communities, forms of social and economic differentiation. That is, while occupying a similar position in the social structure with all fishers, some fishers, as a consequence of a combination of hard work, good fortune, risk-taking, management practices, family background characteristics and numerous other possibilities, achieve a "highliner" status within their occupational and social communities. These producers and their families are usually better off materially as well as being well-regarded socially. While not necessarily liked by most in their occupational fraternity, highline fishers are respected for their know-how and success. As a consequence they often assume unofficial opinion leadership positions within their occupational and social communities, if not active leadership roles in championing their communities' interests.

Such was and is the case for the fishers who initiated fish dragging in Digby Neck and the Islands. Before trying fish dragging they were highline fishers, reputed for their work ethic, risk-taking and management practices. They were engaged in special relationships with fish buyers, in so far as they received marginally higher prices for their fish than did other captains. Certain fish buyers were interested in and supportive of dragging from the beginning. Both parties benefited tremendously from the relationship; one had an enhanced outlet for their catches while the other obtained high volume supply. But, in the process, the reference community for the captains' vested interests switched. They gradually moved out of thorough integration within the fishers' occupational and social communities and became integrated with the fish buyers/processors' community of interests, for the interests and destinies of the dragger captains/owners and the fish buyers/processors were, and remain, inseparably intertwined and allied.

Indeed, several of the earliest and most successful captains/owners participated in joint ventures with local fish buyers/processors, investing in fish weirs, additional vessels and fish companies. A number of these men also started their own fish companies. In short, the advent and adoption of the small boat fish dragger provided the avenue whereby several captains/owners, especially the highline fishers and early entrants, altered their position and that of their families within the local occupational and community social structure. Their interests, their world view, and their practice became allied with and, in many ways, undifferentiated from those of the local fish buyers/processors; they now approach fishing on a growth and profitability basis.

Even more significantly, this shift in the composition of local elites within the social structure reflects the development of fundamental socio-economic differentiations and class divisions within the occupational and social communities of fishers. While wage labour remains rare, increasing numbers of fishers have little choice but to work as crew aboard fish draggers, particularly since the demise of the coastal hook and line fishery. Most of the dragger crew cannot realistically aspire to a captains'/owners' position. The capital wealth necessary for investment in a fish dragger is not available to most. Even if it were, the federal management practice of limited entry licensing ensures that most contemporary crews will not have access to the necessary permits, either as a consequence of the inflationary impact of created scarcity (i.e., limits on numbers) on the cost of licences and/or as a result of sheer unavailability.[5]

In addition to the socio-economic and social structural differentiations and divisions resulting from the above, the remaining small boat hook and line and lobster fishers have become increasingly separated from dragger captains/owners. The local-level, experientially-based, informal rules and practices of the more traditional small boat fisheries are of little, if any, relevance to the dragger fishery. The socio-economic points and frames of reference are both different and at odds with each other. On the one hand, small boat fish dragging is a specialised form of production committed to and dependent upon volume catches and an economic rationality of profitability in a competitive environment. On the other hand, the more traditional small boat fisheries are a generalised system of production reflecting an economic rationality focused on satisfying livelihood goals within locally-referenced, occupational rules and solidarities. Representing conflicting rationalities, the two systems of fish production have been engaged in a struggle from the outset. This struggle, most frequently and superficially described as "gear conflict," concerns the very basis of and solidarity within the occupational and social communities existing on Digby Neck and the Islands. It permeates aspects of socio-economic life and the social dynamics of the occupation, ranging from the determinants of access to crewing positions and qualitative differences in the relative standards of material life, through issue leadership dynamics and community organisation, to patterns of social interaction. To date, this struggle has given rise to the social and economic prominence of dragger captains/owners and a broad-based erosion of the position of fishers working within the more traditional system of production.[6] The consequences of these struggles and shifts for the socio-political dynamics within local occupational and community situations have not been specifically explored here. This requires further study. However, the description and analyses presented certainly suggest that the traditional small boat sector has been reduced to an extent that its potential and ability to marshall the socio-economic resources requisite for effective political pursuit of its interests are rapidly disappearing.

The dilemmas facing the Digby Neck and the Islands fisheries clearly demonstrate the outcomes of existing government policy and the imperatives of increasing capitalisation. Few indicators hold out much hope for the immediate future of this particular fishery. Clearly the capitalised sectors have exceeded the ability of the resource base to support them much longer. As a consequence, several independent dragger captains will lose their enterprises, their ability to fish, and their livelihoods. Initially processors will attempt to respond by purchasing more boats, but some of them will eventually succumb to the cutting edge of unserviceable debt and be forced either out of business or into consolidations. In total, the immediate future of the highly-capitalised sector appears to hold little more than increased concentration of vessel and processing

ownership and decreased employment in fish catching and processing. Given the region's economic dependence upon the fisheries,
these developments would not augur well for the socio-economic
conditions supporting community life. Perhaps the industry will
come full circle; that is, the highly capitalised sector might eventually collapse, leaving the small boat and coastal zone fisheries as the
backbone of the industry. While resulting in some severe difficulties,
such an outcome could permit a qualitative restructuring that would
provide long-term employment benefits, especially when the
resource base began to recover. For this to occur, government and
the major players in industry would have to re-orient their objectives
and roles—a possibility as likely as fish stock regeneration under
the existing conditions.

However, it should be noted that several remedial measures have
the potential to alter the present path of development in a manner
conducive to the regeneration of fish stocks and the socio-economic
vitality of the Digby Neck and the Islands' fishery and communities.
Without question, a quick fix solution is impossible. Any regenera-
tive and substantive public policy intervention would necessarily
have to address the requirements for establishing a sustainable,
humanely and economically sensible basis to the fishery. Such a
goal entails a dramatic reorganisation of the fishery, both locally and
regionally, in concert with changes in the public policy environment
within which the fishery operates. One of the first remedial measures
necessary is the dramatic reduction or elimination of the use of
non-selective, mobile fishing technologies such as otter trawls and
seine nets. This measure would have to be in effect throughout
Atlantic Canada since if it were limited to particular localities, such
as Digby Neck and the Islands, it would have little effect on reducing
exploitative pressures on mobile fish stocks. Non-selective, mobile
fishing technologies, while perhaps economically efficient producers
over the short-term, have been shown in this, as well as other
studies, to result in the over-exploitation and near destruction of
fish stocks. In addition, available evidence suggests that the technical design of some of these technologies, such as otter trawls and
scallop drags, actually destroy marine resource habitats, thereby
limiting the natural regeneration capacities of some species. For
instance, the otter trawl's heavy doors, steel bottom line and rollers
have been shown to tear up the ocean floor —dislodging rocks,
churning up the bottom, ripping asunder plant communities and
disrupting other organic life. Massive disruptions of the ocean floor
habitats of particular marine species can accomplish little but the
destruction of marine resource ecology.[7] Such an outcome is neither

in the interests of marine environments and species nor is it in the interests of the fishers, fish processors and communities dependent upon marine environments and species for their livelihoods.

Ideally, mobile, non-selective and environmentally damaging industrial harvesting technologies should be prohibited. Barring this, their use must be reduced to a fraction of its present application, perhaps defined as permissible only in the limited and strictly managed exploitation of distant water, underutilized species (e.g., silver hake and squid). Mobile, non-selective harvesting technologies might also have some very limited application for the supply of the more commonly sought after species (e.g., cod, haddock and pollock) for resource-short fish plants during the winter months, when inclement weather and/or ice conditions restrict the activity of small boat fishers employing selective and less environmentally damaging technologies such as baited longlines and gill nets. Any extensive use of non-selective, mass harvesting technologies, other than in the instances noted, is tantamount to licensing the rape of marine resources and the destruction of marine ecology.

Of course simple prohibitions or reductions do not solve the problem concerning the future of existing mobile gear fishing capacity. What can and should be done with the large number of small and large vessel draggers, which are specialised fishing platforms in terms of design and economic rationality? The federal and provincial governments, through their departments of fisheries, encouraged the adoption and use of this technology through incentives such as vessel and gear acquisition subsidies and low-interest loans. Consequently, government must bear some financial and technical responsibility for fishers and fish processors in regard to easing the transition from mobile to fixed gear fishing effort. This can be accomplished in a number of ways. For those not prepared to make the transition, the governments should provide a one-time buy back offer: the amount offered should be composed of the balance of the outstanding vessel and equipment loans, plus two years of forgone net income, a figure derived by determining the average net income from the fishing enterprise over the previous five years after deductions for boat shares and operating expenses. Captains/owners opting for this avenue should be required by legal contract to distribute crew shares to full-time crew, as calculated from prior practices, from the total buy-out price. After all, the buy-out of these enterprises eliminates the livelihood of crew as well as captains/owners. Crew livelihoods are derived from agreed upon share divisions of each catch's landed value after the boat's share and operating expense deductions. That is, crew shares are a part of the enterprises total net income and should be treated as such for distribution to crews in buy-out agreements. This approach would relieve owners/captains of enterprise debt burdens and provide all parties with income essential to easing the burden of transition out of the mobile fishery.

For captains/owners committed to adopting fixed gear fishing technologies, the governments should cover the costs of overhauling and refitting vessels. While these vessels are undergoing refit, the governments should cover the costs of outstanding enterprise loans, as well as providing sufficient income support, possibly calculated using the aforementioned buy-out approach, for the captains and full-time crews.

Of course, an attractive refit programme could result in the movement of many fishers and enterprises from the mobile to the fixed gear sectors. This development will not be greeted with unbridled enthusiasm by existing fixed gear fishers. Indeed, many will interpret this approach as yet another benefit for mobile gear owners, owners who have already been the recipients of substantial levels of government support. Existing fixed gear fishers should be provided, at government cost, with a similar opportunity to participate in an upgrading refit in order to assume that they will not be at a competitive disadvantage when the re-tooled mobile gear vessels enter the fixed gear fishery. More importantly, local community and regional committees of existing fixed gear fishers and/or their representatives should be organised and provided with the mandate *to determine* the quantity of new capacity that their fishery can absorb. The provision of either buy-back or refit options to mobile gear enterprise captains/owners should be contingent upon the decisions of these committees, and these committees should determine the quantity and location, for fishing purposes, of new fixed gear capacity. Initiatives such as these would humanely ease transitions within fisheries such as those of Digby Neck and the Islands. Dramatic reductions in non-selective mobile enterprises, could be the basis for the regeneration of marine habitat and stocks necessary to support expanded fixed gear fishing capacity.

The technical qualities of fixed gear technologies will allow for the development of a more selective fishery, while at the same time reducing the level of exploitation. This is assured by the fact that only a limited number of baited hooks and lines or set nets can be fished in any one habitat at a time. Excessive fixed gear fishing in one habitat causes equipment tangles which result in losses and inefficiencies in gear and time, thereby eroding economic viability. Such disincentives place an emphasis among fishers on responsible self-management within local settings of individual as well as total fishing effort and practices. Reductions in landings per unit effort for the refitted mobile vessels should be compensated for by the better prices captains/owners will receive for higher quality fixed gear landings, presuming that port markets respond in recognition of the benefits and value of quality.

In order to assure positive responses in port markets, fish plant buyers and processors should be prohibited from owning and controlling fish catching capacity, as is done for instance in Norway. Conversely, fishers should be prohibited from ownership of fish plants. Such an initiative would facilitate port market price competition for fish landings, particularly high quality landings. This would eventually compel both buyers/processors and fishers to engage in forms of price negotiation and agreement as a way of countervailing the uncertainties and anarchy of unbridled competitive markets. Such a development would benefit both parties.

In the short term, dramatic reduction in mobile fishing effort will reduce supply to processing plants, resulting in unemployment and economic hardship for fish plant workers. The provincial and federal governments should initiate forms of interim income assistance for fish plant workers while the fishery is in transition. Enhanced access to unemployment insurance benefits coupled with employment and training assistance grants to fish plants are but two measures that could be engaged for this purpose. Once the transition is complete and the fish stocks have recovered, supply of premium quality landings should generate more stable, higher income jobs. Premium quality landings will allow fish processors to compete more effectively in the higher value fresh and restaurant markets, while retaining a good portion of the traditional institutional market. Diversification of markets will provide greater employment stability and opportunity, as well as skill acquisition levels demanding higher incomes.

Finally, management of access to and participation in the fishery must be left to those who derive their livelihoods from it—fishers. Fishers are best positioned to know the management interests of their livelihoods. To this end, they must be provided with the decision-making prerogative, and aided by technical assistance and scientific information from government agencies. Once so endowed, fishers will form into the sorts of representative, decision-making organisations which they perceive to be in the best interests of their livelihoods and industry. However, it should be understood that once in the possession of such a prerogative, fishers must live with the decisions they make—no more government bail-outs, no more government intervention to rescue the industry from poor decisions and self-indulgent reasoning.

The above are but a few suggestions for alternatives in the development of fisheries such as those of Digby Neck and the Islands. The intent is to indicate ways in which a more diversified, sustainable, higher value fishery, built upon a healthy marine habitat, can be conceptualised as the objective of, and in the interests of, fishers, fish processors, fish plant workers and the governments alike. Public policy initiatives such as those outlined above require substantial, short-term inputs of public funds. Such is necessarily the case for the industry and those dependent upon it for their livelihoods, if the goal is to realise long-term economic and social stability. Such initiatives should push the industry onto a more sustainable and economically beneficial footing, the sort of footing required for the industry to avoid the cycle of crises inherent in the current path of development. What remains to be seen is whether or not the government can muster the vision and political courage to initiate such dramatic changes.

Many of the current players in the fisheries of Digby Neck and the Islands and elsewhere have themselves yet to demonstrate substantial commitment to a future vision of change in the industry. Many are reported to argue that crises are a consequence of what "the other guy" is doing, failing to recognise themselves as a contributing factor. From this point of view "good" public policy is seen as that which supports one's ability to continue current ways of doing things while compelling "the other guy" to accept profound changes. Indeed, the individualistic utilitarian rationality underwriting most of current fisheries management policy profoundly reinforces and entrenches the narrow-minded, self-interested world view that has lately risen to prominence among fishers, particularly among captains in possession of high value limited entry licences and fish processors committed to high volume, low quality industrial production. These "communities of interests" and their myopic views require exorcism, a process to which most fishers and fishing communities have shown little commitment. Perhaps deep crisis and jeopardy are the crucibles in which the necessary vision will be forged and the resolve formed to pursue the development of a sustainable fishery. Hopefully, crisis and jeopardy can be anticipated, enabling effective interventions *before* the costs to human lives and communities escalate. For the people of Digby Neck and the Islands, the costs have already begun to mount. Building a sustainable fishery is a present-day necessity, not a futuristic muse. As an elder captain observed:

You've got to hope there'll be lots of jobs in tourism because the way things look now, showing tourists what it used to be like fishin' is all that'll be left us. Either that or movin' out.

Appendix

Labour Force 15 Years and Over by Industry Division by Sex for Digby Neck and the Islands Community Areas,[1] 1981

Industry Division	Community Areas					
	Centreville—Sandy Cove			Little River—East Ferry		
	Male	Female	Total	Male	Female	Total
	%	%	N	%	%	N
Agriculture	50.0	50.0	10	100.0	-	5
Forestry	-	-	-	-	-	-
Fishing and Trapping	100.0	-	10	100.0	-	60
Mines	-	-	-	-	-	-
Manufacturing	66.7	33.3	45	72.8	22.2	45
Construction	100.0	-	15	-	-	-
Transportation, Communication and Other Utilities	-	100.0	5	50.0	50.0	20
Trade	50.0	50.0	10	25.0	75.0	40
Finance, Insurance and Real Estate	-	100.0	5	-	-	-
Community, Business and Personal Service	-	100.0	20	100.0	-	10
Public Administration and Defense	66.7	33.3	15	-	-	-
Industry Unspecified	-	-	-	100.0	0	15
TOTAL	63.6	36.4	135	74.4	25.6	195

Cont'd

1. Community Areas correspond with Statistics Canada Ennumeration Areas. The data provided by Statistics Canada is based on a 20 percent sample and rounded to the next highest unit of five.

Cont'd from previous page.

Industry Division	Community Areas					
	Tiverton			**Freeport**		
	Male %	Female %	Total N	Male %	Female %	Total N
Agriculture	-	-	-	-	-	-
Forestry	-	-	-	-	-	-
Fishing and Trapping	100.0	-	40	100.0	-	45
Mines	-	-	-	-	-	-
Manufacturing	50.0	50.0	40	50.0	50.0	80
Construction	-	-	-	100.0	-	10
Transportation, Communication and Other Utilities	100.0	-	10	50.0	50.0	10
Trade	75.0	25.0	20	25.0	75.0	20
Finance, Insurance and Real Estate	-	-	-	-	100.0	10
Community, Business and Personal Service	-	100.0	5	50.0	50.0	50
Public Administration and Defense	160.0	40.0	25	-		--
Industry Unspecified	-	-	-	-	-	-
TOTAL	71.4	28.6	140	57.8	42.2	225

Cont'd

Cont'd from previous page.

Industry Division	Community Areas Westport			Total, all areas		
	Male %	Female %	Total N	Male %	Female %	Total N
Agriculture	-	-		-	67.7	33.3
Forestry	-	-	-	-	-	-
Fishing and Trapping	88.9	11.1	45	97.8	2.2	200
Mines	-	-	-	-	-	-
Manufacturing	85.7	14.3	35	63.3	36.7	245
Construction	100.0	-	10	100.0	-	35
Transportation, Communication and Other Utilities	100.0	-	10	63.6	36.4	55
Trade	100.0	-	10	45.0	55.0	100
Finance, Insurance and Real Estate	-	-	-	-	100.0	15
Community, Business and Personal Service	-	100.0	10	36.8	63.2	95
Public Administration and Defense	100.0	-	5	75.0	25.0	45
Industry Unspecified	100.0	-	5	77.8	22.2	20
TOTAL	80.8	19.2	130	69.0	31.0	825

Source: Statistics Canada, Census of Canada. SP12FEDO11EA207-211.

Notes

Preface

1. For examples of this view see: Copes 1980; Copes 1983; and *Task Force on Atlantic Fisheries.*
2. The preliminary findings of this research project are reported in Apostle, *et al.* 1985.
3. Hughes *et al.* 1960.

Chapter 1

1. Pseudonyms are used throughout this volume.
2. A much condensed version of this volume, titled, "Modernisation and the Dilemmas of Technological Change in a Fishery: The Case of Digby Neck and the Islands" will appear in *Land and Sea: Uneven Development and Capitalist Differentiation in the Fishing Industry* (R. Apostle and G. Barrett, eds.). This book, now in preparation, contains a compilation of the research findings from the SSHRCC-funded project that supported the inquiry reported on in this volume.

Chapter 2

1. For convenience I will use the term Digby Neck and the Islands to cover the whole area. The research covered the areas from Brier Island to Centreville.
2. For a more detailed discussion of these phenomena see Apostle *et al.* 1985.

Chapter 3

1. Such practices are common to fishing peoples and have been widely noted by researchers. For a review of this literature see Acheson 1981:275–316.

2. Property claims of this sort and their impact upon the organisation of coastal zone fishing have been described and discussed by a number of researchers. See Acheson 1975:183–207; Andersen 1979:299–336; Davis 1984:133–165. This documentation draws into question the accuracy of the federal government policy perspective that marine resources are common property. This perspective argues that the fundamental problem confronting the development of an economically rational industry is simply the tendency for fishers in common property circumstances to over-exploit resources. Little incentive exists to husband and to preserve common property resources. Every fisher, in direct competition with every other fisher will be motivated to take as much resource as he/she can, as frequently as possible. It is argued that this condition leads to resource over-exploitation and the socio-economic problem of too many fishers pursing too few fish. For a more detailed exposition of the common property perspective see: Gordon 1954:124–42; Clark 1981:231–237; Environment Canada, Fisheries and Marine Service, *Policy for Canada's Commercial Fisheries* 1976:39ff.; Scott and Neher 1982:1–9; and *Task Force on Atlantic Fisheries* 1982:211ff. Contrary to this perspective, a growing body of information regarding informal, local-level systems of access control and management suggests that the character of the imperatives driving productive activity is more closely linked to over-exploitation than simple assumptions concerning human activity in common property environments. That is, productive activities determined to maximise returns will have a different impact on resources than will activities focused on livelihood goals.

3. For data verifying this see: Charron 1977; Davis 1984:251ff.

4. The captive feature is recognised as a characteristic of labour forces in single industry communities, cf. *Task Force on Atlantic Fisheries* 1982:97–98.

5. The owners of two of these plants recently purchased the National Sea Products plant in Digby Town.

Chapter 4

1. I am not claiming that small draggers were first developed in the Digby Neck area of Nova Scotia. Small draggers were reported at about the same time in the Yarmouth area and around Grand Manan Island. Moreover, smaller-sized draggers had been employed by American fishers several years earlier. My focus here is on the events surrounding the adoption and development of dragger technologies in the Digby Neck and Islands fishery.

2. The quantified information and quotations provided hereafter, unless otherwise specified, were obtained from summaries of the annual *Narrative Reports* submitted every year by a fisheries officer located in the Digby Neck and Islands area (Fisheries District 37). He was given a list of subject areas in which I was particularly interested. The

information provided has proven indispensable to my understanding of the Digby Neck and the Islands fishery.

3. By now this hull type was being built in boat shops throughout the Digby-Yarmouth county areas, not just at Cape St. Mary's.

Chapter 5

1. These reports are derived from summaries of the *Narrative Reports* submitted by District 37 fisheries officers to federal authorities at the end of every calendar year.

2. Notably the same types of complaints were made by weir fishers concerning herring seiners and by hook and line fishers regarding pollock seining operations.

3. For detailed and informative discussion of these events and their consequences for fisheries development see: Barrett 1979:127–160 and Barrett 1984:77–104.

4. Pollock were being seined during the '60s, and increases in their landings through this period are not arguably associated with drag fishing. However, the intensification of the exploitation of pollock is directly connected with the use of more technically sophisticated and costly fishing technologies. One District 37 fisheries officer reported in 1962 that hook and line fishers were upset with the government for permitting seiners to fish pollock.

5. Several informants report that it was common to record haddock landings as pollock because of the extremely low landings permissible under federal government quota regulations. This would explain the jump in pollock landings reported through this period.

6. Biologists have been warning the Department of Fisheries and Oceans of a pending crisis in this regard. New, very low, haddock quotas were set for 1985 in the Scotia-Fundy Region as a countermeasure. However, recent fisher and fish buyer opposition to this has re-opened the question.

7. Actual weights can be derived by applying these percentages to the landings data for District 37 presented in Table 6. It must be noted that, for statistical purposes, the Department of Fisheries and Oceans classifies all fish landed in vessels under 25 gross tonnes as inshore catches. There are a number of boats in this category that actually fish offshore grounds. Conversely, a number of the vessels over 25 gross tonnes that have their catches categorised as offshore, regularly fish inshore grounds. However, the most of the line fishing effort is captured by the inshore category. For a description and discussion of inshore/ offshore categories see Davis *et al.* 1983.

8. Dependence upon one fishery, especially a closely regulated fishery such as lobster fishing, can result in many difficulties for both the fishers and federal fisheries officers. While catches remain high there is little likelihood that problems will surface. But, once they begin

dropping, as they will, income needs will motivate increasing numbers of persons to engage in activities such as poaching and working traps in excess of the number permissible by regulations.

9. Determined by dividing the totalled landed weights for 1952 and 1983 given in Table 6, by the total number of fishers fishing in 1952 and 1983 provided in Table 5.

Chapter 6

1. There is an extensive literature on the characteristics and consequences of fisher/fish buyer debt-obligation relationships. For instance, see: Antler and Faris 1979:129–154; Barrett 1982; Faris 1977:235–251; Ommer 1981:107–124; Williams 1978:29–33.

2. This fact is resoundingly established by the investigations of the Royal Commission on Price Spreads concerning the mechanisms reflected in the difference between what producers received and what consumers paid for fish during the '50s. See *Price Spreads of Food Products*. Vol. 1 and 2. Ottawa: Queen's Printer 1959.

Chapter 7

1. A condensed version of some of the material presented in this chapter appears in Davis and Thiessen 1988.

2. These figures are calculated from data presented in Mitchell and Frick 1970:36.

3. For examples of the gear conflict argument see *Task Force on Atlantic Fisheries* 1982:31–43.

4. See Barrett 1984, for a comprehensive description and analysis of this process.

5. Further illustrations and discussion of this conflict is presented in Davis 1984.

6. For a more developed, empirically-supported analysis of these points see: Davis and Thiessen 1986; and Thiessen and Davis 1986.

7. Personal communication, Halifax Office, Unemployment Insurance.

8. The conditions confronting many coastal zone fishers are even more problematic when one includes consideration of their capital debt position in regard to federal and provincial boat construction and equipment purchase financing programmes. In short, specialisation and income dependence on government transfers are not conditions likely to improve fishers' ability to repay government held loans. For more detailed discussion of these aspects of the relation between government and fishers see: Davis and Kasdan 1984; and *Task Force on Atlantic Fisheries* 1982:74–78.

Chapter 8

1. For an example of this see Environment Canada, Fisheries and Marine Service 1976.

2. For examples, see Davis and Kasdan 1984; and *Task Force on Atlantic Fisheries* 1982.

3. There is a very developed literature and debate concerned with the capitalisation of primary production and the penetration by capital of petty commodity forms of production. For an example of this see: Goodman and Redclift 1981; and Mann and Dickinson 1978.

4. In October, 1987 one of these processors absorbed the other. This same processor had earlier (1985) purchased the Digby plant from National Sea Products. From a very modest beginning, this independent, locally-owned fish business has become the predominant buyer/processor in the Digby Neck and the Islands region as well as a major player within the Nova Scotia fishing industry. Notably, these developments are consistent with our prediction that the dilemma of dependence on fish dragging in an environment of stock collapse would result in further consolidation of fish processing in the region.

5. Limited entry licensing inflates the "market" value of high-demand, available permits. In cases such as lobster and other trawl licences, the "value" (cost) of the licence adds tens of thousands of dollars on to the capital costs of the enterprises. For a more detailed discussion and analysis of this see Davis and Thiessen 1988 and Thiessen and Davis 1988.

6. Processes and outcomes similar to the ones covered here have been noted by Peter Sinclair in his study of the northwest Newfoundland fisheries (Sinclair 1983 and Sinclair 1985).

7. Personal communication, Fisheries Technology Branch, Department of Fisheries and Oceans. Halifax, May 1989.

References

Acheson, James M. 1975 "The Lobster Fiefs: Economic and Ecological Effects of Territoriality in the Marine Lobster Fishery." *Human Ecology*, 3:183–207.

_____ 1981 "Anthropology of Fishing." *Annual Review of Anthropology*, 10:275–316.

Andersen, Raoul 1978 "The Need for Human Science Research in Atlantic Coast Fisheries." *Journal of the Fisheries Research Board of Canada*, 35(7):1031–1049.

_____ 1979 "Public and Private Access Management in Newfoundland Fishing." In R. Andersen (ed.), *North American Maritime Communities: Anthropological Essays on Changing Adaptations*. The Hague: Mouton Publishers.

Alexander, David 1977 *The Decay of Trade: An Economic History of the Newfoundland Salt Fish Trade, 1935–1965*. St. John's: Institute of Social and Economic Research, Memorial University of Newfoundland.

Antler, Ellen and James Faris 1979 "Adaptation to Changes in Technology and Government Policy: A Newfoundland Example (Cat Harbour)." In R. Andersen (ed.), *North Atlantic Maritime Cultures: Anthropological Essays on Changing Adaptations*. The Hague: Mouton Publishers.

Apostle, Richard, L. Gene Barrett, Anthony Davis and Leonard Kasdan 1985 "Land and Sea: The Structure of Fish Processing in Nova Scotia, A Preliminary Report." Research Report. Gorsebrook Research Institute, St. Mary's University. Halifax, Nova Scotia.

Baker, D. 1979 *Who Benefits From Fishing Vessel Construction Subsidies?* A Report prepared for the Department of Fisheries and Oceans, Government of Canada. Halifax, Nova Scotia.

Barrett, L. Gene 1979 "Underdevelopment and Social Movements in the Nova Scotia Fishing Industry to 1938." In Robert J. Brym and R. James Sacouman (eds.), *Underdevelopment and Social Movements in Atlantic Canada*. Toronto: Hogtown Press.

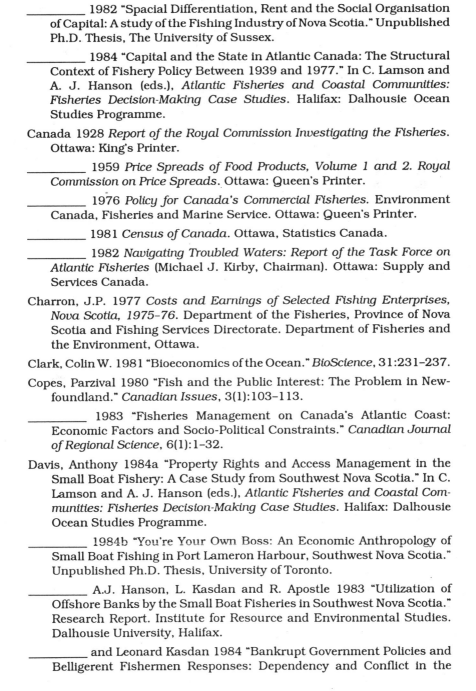

_____ 1982 "Spacial Differentiation, Rent and the Social Organisation of Capital: A study of the Fishing Industry of Nova Scotia." Unpublished Ph.D. Thesis, The University of Sussex.

_____ 1984 "Capital and the State in Atlantic Canada: The Structural Context of Fishery Policy Between 1939 and 1977." In C. Lamson and A. J. Hanson (eds.), *Atlantic Fisheries and Coastal Communities: Fisheries Decision-Making Case Studies*. Halifax: Dalhousie Ocean Studies Programme.

Canada 1928 *Report of the Royal Commission Investigating the Fisheries*. Ottawa: King's Printer.

_____ 1959 *Price Spreads of Food Products, Volume 1 and 2. Royal Commission on Price Spreads*. Ottawa: Queen's Printer.

_____ 1976 *Policy for Canada's Commercial Fisheries*. Environment Canada, Fisheries and Marine Service. Ottawa: Queen's Printer.

_____ 1981 *Census of Canada*. Ottawa, Statistics Canada.

_____ 1982 *Navigating Troubled Waters: Report of the Task Force on Atlantic Fisheries* (Michael J. Kirby, Chairman). Ottawa: Supply and Services Canada.

Charron, J.P. 1977 *Costs and Earnings of Selected Fishing Enterprises, Nova Scotia, 1975–76*. Department of the Fisheries, Province of Nova Scotia and Fishing Services Directorate. Department of Fisheries and the Environment, Ottawa.

Clark, Colin W. 1981 "Bioeconomics of the Ocean." *BioScience*, 31:231–237.

Copes, Parzival 1980 "Fish and the Public Interest: The Problem in Newfoundland." *Canadian Issues*, 3(1):103–113.

_____ 1983 "Fisheries Management on Canada's Atlantic Coast: Economic Factors and Socio-Political Constraints." *Canadian Journal of Regional Science*, 6(1):1–32.

Davis, Anthony 1984a "Property Rights and Access Management in the Small Boat Fishery: A Case Study from Southwest Nova Scotia." In C. Lamson and A. J. Hanson (eds.), *Atlantic Fisheries and Coastal Communities: Fisheries Decision-Making Case Studies*. Halifax: Dalhousie Ocean Studies Programme.

_____ 1984b "You're Your Own Boss: An Economic Anthropology of Small Boat Fishing in Port Lameron Harbour, Southwest Nova Scotia." Unpublished Ph.D. Thesis, University of Toronto.

_____ A.J. Hanson, L. Kasdan and R. Apostle 1983 "Utilization of Offshore Banks by the Small Boat Fisheries in Southwest Nova Scotia." Research Report. Institute for Resource and Environmental Studies. Dalhousie University, Halifax.

_____ and Leonard Kasdan 1984 "Bankrupt Government Policies and Belligerent Fishermen Responses: Dependency and Conflict in the

Southwest Nova Scotian Small Boat Fisheries." *Journal of Canadian Studies*, 19(1):108–124.

_____ and Victor Thiessen 1986 "Making Sense of the Dollars: Income Distribution Among Atlantic Canadian fishermen and Public Policy." *Marine Policy*, 10(3):201–214.

_____ and Victor Thiessen 1988 "Public Policy and Social Control in the Atlantic Fisheries." *Canadian Public Policy*, XIV:66–77.

Deveau, J.A. 1977 *Along the Shores of St. Mary's Bay: The Story of a Unique Community*. Churchpoint: College of St. Anne Press.

Faris, James 1977 "Primitive Accumulation in Small-Scale Fishing Communities." In M Estellie Smith (ed.), *Those Who Live From The Sea: A Study in Maritime Anthropology*. American Ethnological Society. Monograph 62. St. Paul: West Publishing Company.

Goodman, David and Michael Redclift 1981 *From Peasant to Proletarian: Capitalist Development and Agrarian Transitions*. Oxford: Basil Blackwell.

Gordon, Scott H. 1954 "The Economic Theory of a Common-Property Resource: The Fishery." *Journal of Political Economy*, 62:124–42.

Hare, G.M. 1977 *Atlas of the Major Atlantic Coast Fish and Invertebrate Resources Adjacent to the Canada-United States Boundary Areas*. Technical Report No. 681. Department of the Environment, Fisheries and Marine Service.

Hichley, J.D., D.B. Cann and J.I. MacDougall 1962 *Soil Survey of Digby County, Nova Scotia, Canada*. Department of Agriculture. Ottawa: Queen's Printer.

Hughes, C.C., M.A. Trembly, M.A. Rapport and A.H. Leighton 1960 *People of Cove and Woodlot*. New York: Basic Books Inc.

Jensen, L.B. 1980 *Fishermen of Nova Scotia*. Halifax: Petheric Press Limited.

Kearney, John F. 1984 *Working Together: A Study of Fishermen's Responses to Government Management of the District 4A Lobster Fishery*. Universite Sainte-Anne, Nova Scotia.

Macdonald, R.D.S. 1984 "Canadian Fisheries Policy and the Development of Atlantic Coast Groundfisheries Management." In C. Lamson and A.J. Hanson (eds.), *Atlantic Fisheries and Coastal Communities: Fisheries Decision-Making Class Studies*. Halifax: Dalhousie Ocean Studies Programme.

MacPherson, William J. 1976 *In List Of Fish Processors in Nova Scotia*. Fisheries Statistics and Computer Services Division. Fisheries and Marine Service, Department of the Environment. Halifax, Nova Scotia.

Mann, Susan A. and James M. Dickinson 1978 "Obstacles to the Development of a Capitalist Agriculture." *Journal of Peasant Studies*, 5(4):467–481.

Mitchell, C.C. and H.C. Frick 1970 *Government Programs of Assistance for Fishing Craft Construction in Canada: An Economic Appraisal.* Canadian Fisheries Reports No. 14. Economic Branch, Fisheries Service, Department of Fisheries and Forestry. Ottawa: Information Canada.

Ommer, Rosemary E. 1981 "'All the Fish of the Past,' Property Resource Rights and Development in a Nineteenth Century Inshore Fishery." *Acadiensis,* 10(2):107–124.

Province of Nova Scotia 1978 *Port Profiles.* Department of Fisheries, Province of Nova Scotia, Halifax, Nova Scotia.

Richardson, Stephen A. 1952 "Technological Change: Some Effects on Three Canadian Fishing Villages." *Human Organisation,* 11(3):17–27.

Scotia-Fundy Lobster Fishing Working Committee 1989 *The Scotia-Fundy Lobster Fishery. Working Committee Draft Report for Industry Consultation.* Department of Fisheries and Oceans, Halifax, Nova Scotia.

Scott, Anthony and Philip A. Neher 1982 *The Public Regulation of Commercial Fisheries in Canada: A Study Prepared for the Economic Council of Canada.* Ottawa, Canada.

Sinclair, Peter 1983 "'Fishermen Divided': The Impact of Limited Entry Licensing in Northwest Newfoundland." *Human Organisation,* 42(4):307–314.

_____ 1985 *From Traps to Draggers: Domestic Commodity Production in Northwest Newfoundland.* St. John's: Institute of Social and Economic Research.

Thiessen, Victor and Anthony Davis 1986 "A Further Note to Making Sense of the Dollars: Income Distribution Among Atlantic Canadian Fishermen and Public Policy." *Marine Policy,* 10(4):310–314.

_____ and Anthony Davis 1988 "Recruitment to Small Boat Fishing and Public Policy in the Atlantic Canadian Fisheries." *Canadian Review of Sociology and Anthropology.*

Williams, Rick 1978 "Nova Scotia: Fish At My Price Or Don't Fish." *Canadian Dimension,* 10(2):29–33.

ISER BOOKS

Studies

43 **Dire Straits: The Dilemmas of a Fishery: The Case of Digby Neck and the Islands**—Anthony Davis

42 **Saying Isn't Believing: Conversational Narrative and the Discourse of Tradition in a French-Newfoundland Community**—Gary R. Butler

41 **A Place in the Sun: Shetland and Oil—Myths and Realities**—Jonathan Wills

40 **The Native Game: Settler Perceptions of Indian/Settler Relations in Central Labrador**—Evelyn Plaice

39 **The Northern Route: An Ethnography of Refugee Experiences**—Lisa Gilad

38 **Hostage to Fortune: Bantry Bay and the Encounter with Gulf Oil**—Chris Eipper

37 **Language and Poverty: The Persistence of Scottish Gaelic in Eastern Canada**—Gilbert Foster

36 **A Public Nuisance: A History of the Mummers Troupe**—Chris Brookes

35 **Listen While I Tell You: A Story of the Jews of St. John's, Newfoundland**—Alison Kahn

34 **Talking Violence: An Anthropological Interpretation of Conversation in the City**—Nigel Rapport

33 **"To Each His Own": William Coaker and the Fishermen's Protective Union in Newfoundland Politics, 1908–1925**—Ian D.H. McDonald, edited by J.K Hiller

32 **Sea Change: A Shetland Society, 1970–79**—Reginald Byron

31 **From Traps to Draggers: Domestic Commodity Production in Northwest Newfoundland, 1850–1982**—Peter Sinclair

30 **The Challenge of Oil: Newfoundland's Quest for Controlled Development**—J.D. House

29 **Sons and Seals: A Voyage to the Ice**—Guy Wright

28 **Blood and Nerves: An Ethnographic Focus on Menopause**—Dona Lee Davis

27 **Holding the Line: Ethnic Boundaries in a Northern Labrador Community**—John Kennedy

26 **'Power Begins at the Cod End': The Newfoundland Trawlermen's Strike, 1974–75**—David Macdonald

25 **Terranova: The Ethos and Luck of Deep-Sea Fishermen**—Joseba Zulaika (in Canada only)

24 **"Bloody Decks and a Bumper Crop": The Rhetoric of Sealing Counter-Protest**—Cynthia Lamson

23 **Bringing Home Animals: Religious Ideology and Mode of Production of the Mistassini Cree Hunters**—Adrian Tanner (in Canada only)

22 **Bureaucracy and World View: Studies in the Logic of Official Interpretation**—Don Handelman and Elliott Leyton

21 **If You Don't Be Good: Verbal Social Control in Newfoundland**—John Widdowson

20 **You Never Know What They Might Do: Mental Illness in Outport Newfoundland**—Paul S. Dinham

19 **The Decay of Trade: An Economic History of the Newfoundland Saltfish Trade, 1935–1965**—David Alexander

18 **Manpower and Educational Development in Newfoundland**—S.S. Mensinkai and M.Q. Dalvi

17 **Ancient People of Port au Choix: The Excavation of an Archaic Indian Cemetery in Newfoundland**—James A. Tuck

16 **Cain's Land Revisited: Culture Change in Central Labrador, 1775–1972**—David Zimmerly

15 **The One Blood: Kinship and Class in an Irish Village**—Elliott Leyton

14 **The Management of Myths: The Politics of Legitimation in a Newfoundland Community**—A.P. Cohen (in North America only)

13 **Beluga Hunters: An Archaeological Reconstruction of the History and Culture of the Mackenzie Delta Kittegaryumiut**—Robert McGhee

12 **Hunters in the Barrens: The Naskapi on the Edge of the White Man's World**—Georg Henriksen

11 **Now, Whose Fault is That? The Struggle for Self-Esteem in the Face of Chronic Unemployment**—Cato Wadel

10 **Craftsman-Client Contracts: Interpersonal Relations in a Newfoundland Fishing Community**—Louis Chiaramonte

9 **Newfoundland Fishermen in the Age of Industry: A Sociology of Economic Dualism**—Ottar Brox

8 **Public Policy and Community Protest: The Fogo Case**—Robert L. DeWitt

7 **Marginal Adaptations and Modernization in Newfoundland: A Study of Strategies and Implications of Resettlement and Redevelopment of Outport Fishing Communities**—Cato Wadel

6 **Communities in Decline: An Examination of Household Resettlement in Newfoundland**—N. Iverson and D. Ralph Matthews

5 **Brothers and Rivals: Patrilocality in Savage Cove**—Melvin Firestone

4 **Makkovik: Eskimos and Settlers in a Labrador Community**—Shmuel Ben-Dor

3 **Cat Harbour: A Newfoundland Fishing Settlement**—James C. Faris

2 **Private Cultures and Public Imagery: Interpersonal Relations in a Newfoundland Peasant Society**—John F. Szwed

1 **Fisherman, Logger, Merchant, Miner: Social Change and Industrialism in Three Newfoundland Communities**—Tom Philbrook

Papers

18 **To Work and to Weep: Women in Fishing Economies**—Jane Nadel-Klein and Dona Lee Davis (eds.)

17 **A Question of Survival: The Fisheries and Newfoundland Society**—Peter R. Sinclair (ed.)

16 **Fish Versus Oil: Resources and Rural Development in North Atlantic Societies**—J.D. House (ed.)

15 **Advocacy and Anthropology: First Encounters**—Robert Paine (ed.)

14 **Indigenous Peoples and the Nation-State: Fourth World Politics in Canada, Australia and Norway**—Noel Dyck (ed.)

13 **Minorities and Mother Country Imagery**—Gerald Gold (ed.)

12 **The Politics of Indianness: Case Studies of Native Ethnopolitics in Canada**—Adrian Tanner (ed.)

11 **Belonging: Identity and Social Organisation in British Rural Cultures**—Anthony P. Cohen (ed.) (in North America only)

10 **Politically Speaking: Cross-Cultural Studies of Rhetoric**—Robert Paine (ed.)

 9 **A House Divided? Anthropological Studies of Factionalism**—M. Silverman and R.F. Salisbury (eds.)

 8 **The Peopling of Newfoundland: Essays in Historical Geography**—John J. Mannion (ed.)

 7 **The White Arctic: Anthropological Essays on Tutelage and Ethnicity**—Robert Paine (ed.)

 6 **Consequences of Offshore Oil and Gas—Norway, Scotland and Newfoundland**—M.J. Scarlett (ed.)

 5 **North Atlantic Fishermen: Anthropological Essays on Modern Fishing**—Raoul Andersen and Cato Wadel (eds.)

 4 **Intermediate Adaptation in Newfoundland and the Arctic: A Strategy of Social and Economic Development**—Milton M.R. Freeman (ed.)

 3 **The Compact: Selected Dimensions of Friendship**—Elliott Leyton (ed.)

 2 **Patrons and Brokers in the East Arctic**—Robert Paine (ed.)

 1 **Viewpoints on Communities in Crisis**—Michael L. Skolnik (ed.)

Mailing Address:
ISER Books (Institute of Social and Economic Research)
Memorial University of Newfoundland
St. John's, Newfoundland, Canada, A1C 5S7

Printed in Canada